ECOLOGICAL ECONOMICS AND
THE ECOLOGY OF ECONOMICS

Ecological Economics and the Ecology of Economics

Essays in Criticism

Herman E. Daly

Professor, School of Public Affairs,
University of Maryland, USA

Edward Elgar
Cheltenham, UK • Northampton, MA, USA

Published by
Edward Elgar Publishing Limited
Glensanda House
Montpellier Parade
Cheltenham
Glos GL50 1UA
UK

Edward Elgar Publishing, Inc.
136 West Street
Suite 202
Northampton
Massachusetts 01060
USA

A catalogue record for this book
is available from the British Library

Library of Congress Cataloguing in Publication Data

Daly, Herman E.
    Ecological economics and the ecology of economics : essays in criticism / Herman E. Daly.
    Includes bibliographical references.
    1. Environmental economics   I. Title.
    HC79.E5D3243 1999
    333.7—dc21   98–53414
                                                                       CIP

ISBN 1 85898 968 X (cased)

Printed and bound in Great Britain by Biddles Ltd, Guildford and King's Lynn

Contents

PART VI   ON MONEY

PART VII   ON PURPOSE

Figures

Acknowledgements

The publishers wish to thank the following who have kindly given permission for the use of copyright material.

Academic Press Inc. for article: 'Comment: Is the entropy law relevant to the economics of natural resource scarcity? – Yes, of course it is!', *Journal of Environmental Economics and Management*, **23**, July 1992, pp. 91–5.

Association for Evolutionary Economics for article: 'Chicago School individualism versus sexual reproduction: a critique of Becker and Tomes', *Journal of Economic Issues*, March 1982, pp. 307–12.

Association for Social Sciences for article: 'Review of Edward O. Wilson's *On Human Nature*', *Review of Social Economy*, October 1979, pp. 241–4.

Beacon Press for article: 'Money, debt, and wealth', modified Afterword from Herman E. Daly and John B. Cobb, Jr, *For the Common Good: Redirecting the Economy toward community, the environment, and a sustainable future*, 2nd edition, 1994, pp. 407–42.

Blackwell Scientific Publications Inc. for article: 'Beginning again on purpose', *Conservation Biology*, **7** (3), September 1993, pp 736–8.

Critical Review for article: 'Free market environmentalism: turning a good servant into a bad master', *Critical Review*, **6** (2–3), 1993, pp. 171–83.

Elsevier Science for articles: 'Ultimate confusion: the economics of Julian Simon', *Futures*, **17** (5), October 1985, pp. 446–50; 'Review of Martin W. Lewis's *Green Delusions: an environmentalist critique of radical environmentalism*', Duke University Press, 1992 in *Ecological Economics*, **9** (2), February 1994; 'Georgescu-Roegen versus Solow/Stiglitz', *Ecological Economics*, **22** (3), September 1997, pp. 261–6 and 'Reply to Solow/Stiglitz', *Ecological Economics*, **22** (3), September 1997, pp. 271–3.

Ford House for article: 'The cosmic purpose', *Resurgence*, July/August 1996.

Island Press for article 'Boundless Bull' in Craig L. LaMay and Everette E. Dennis (eds), *Media and the Environment*, 1991, pp. 149–55.

The Population Council for articles: 'Review of Wilfred Beckerman's *Small is Stupid: Blowing the Whistle on the Greens*', *Population and Development Review*, **21** (3), September 1995, pp. 665–73 and '*Population Growth and Economic Development: Policy Questions* – a review', special review symposium in *Population and Development Review*, **12** (3), September 1986, pp. 582–5.

Pluto Press for article: 'Farewell lecture to the World Bank', chapter 9 in John Cavanagh et al. (eds), *Beyond Bretton Woods: Alternative to the global economic order*, 1994, pp. 109–17.

United Nations Publications for article: 'Free trade, sustainable development and growth: some serious contradictions – a review' being a review of 'International policies to accelerate sustainable development', Chapter I, Section I of Agenda 21 of the United Nations Conference on Environment and Development for the Centre for Our Common Future, 1992.

The University of Wisconsin Press for article: 'Thermodynamic and economic concepts as related to resource-use policies: comment', *Land Economics*, **6** (3), August 1986, pp. 319–22.

Every effort has been made to trace all the copyright holders but if any have been inadvertently overlooked the publishers will be pleased to make the necessary arrangements at the first opportunity.

Biographical sketch

Herman E. Daly is currently Professor at the University of Maryland, School of Public Affairs. From 1988 to 1994 he was Senior Economist in the Environment Department of the World Bank. Prior to 1988 he was Alumni Professor of Economics at Louisiana State University, where he taught economics for twenty years. He holds a B.A. from Rice University and a Ph.D. from Vanderbilt University. He has served as Ford Foundation Visiting Professor at the University of Ceará (Brazil), as a Research Associate at Yale University, as a Visiting Fellow at the Australian National University, and as a Senior Fulbright Lecturer in Brazil. He has served on the boards of directors of numerous environmental organizations, including the International Society for Ecological Economics, the Beijer Ecological Economics Institute of the Swedish Royal Academy of Sciences and the WorldWatch Institute, and he is co-founder and associate editor of the journal *Ecological Economics*. His interest in economic development, population, resources and environment has resulted in over one hundred articles in professional journals and anthologies, as well as numerous books, including *Toward a Steady-State Economy* (1973); *Steady-State Economics* (1977, 1991); *Valuing the Earth* (1993); and *Beyond Growth* (1996). He is co-author with theologian John B. Cobb, Jr of *For the Common Good* (1989, 1994) which received the 1991 Grawemeyer Award for Ideas for Improving World Order. In 1996 he received the Honorary Right Livelihood Award ('alternative Nobel prize'), and the Heineken Prize for Environmental Science awarded by the Royal Netherlands Academy of Arts and Sciences.

Introduction

Ecological economics has now had more than a decade of existence and development in its modern form – much longer if one traces its historical roots.[1] Its distinguishing characteristic is that it sees the economy as a subsystem of a larger ecosystem that is finite, non-growing, and materially closed, while open to a flow-through (throughput) of solar energy that is also finite and non-growing. The biophysical constraints of the larger system upon the economic subsystem, and the co-evolving mutual adaptations by both systems to those constraints, is the subject matter of ecological economics.

But what is meant by 'the ecology of economics'? What I have in mind are the competitive and symbiotic relations between different species of economists – microeconomists, macroeconomists, international trade specialists, monetary economists, development economists, welfare economists – and especially the competition and symbiosis between ecological economists and all those branches of standard neoclassical economics just listed. The basic viewpoint of ecological economics has challenging implications for these specific fields. Exactly what these implications are, and how they fare in the struggle for existence among ideas, is a part of the 'ecology of economics'.

Standard neoclassical economics has become a brittle, desiccated and ossified discipline. No longer does the university student of economics get any exposure to the history of economic thought, or to economic history, or to comparative economic systems (capitalism, communism, socialism). All systems other than capitalism are thought to have failed; modern capitalism is triumphant, so other systems at other times are considered irrelevant. No alternatives to the here and now find any place in the curriculum. The only issue addressed is fine-tuning the efficiency of modern capitalism, and that is the job of 'value-neutral' neoclassical economics. Like an overadapted ecosystem, the economy has become brittle, and, under the tutelage of economists, has sacrificed purpose for a socially blind, short-run, mechanistic concept of efficiency. The last section of this book returns to the theme of purpose.

The essays in this book are critical, sometimes polemical. If you think the house is on fire then it is inappropriate not to shout. I do not believe in calling people names, but I do believe in naming the people who are calling for the wrong policies. It is people who put ideas into practice, and we all have a responsibility for the correctness and the consequences of the ideas we advocate. I have received my share of criticism from other economists, and I can say from experience that I much prefer to be directly criticized by name, with citations to my offending words, than to be anonymously and 'charitably' dismissed as a 'well-meaning but misguided critic of economic growth'. This kind of criticism often passes as scholarly avoidance of conflict, but in fact allows my critic to attribute anything vaguely to 'me', without incurring any responsibility, and without giving the reader a chance to verify a reference. So I will try to do unto others as I would have them do unto me.

Of course it is no good just criticizing ideas proposed by others if one has nothing positive to offer. But neither is it worthwhile to offer a positive alternative if there is nothing wrong with the prevailing orthodoxy. The positive vision of ecological economics is evident in these essays, and has been developed more fully elsewhere. Nevertheless, the emphasis here is unapologetically, and sometimes aggressively, critical.

Historically economic theory developed in a context of controversy – is value determined by labour or by marginal utility? Is rent price-determining or price-determined? Is a government deficit a good or bad policy in a depression? Are protective tariffs good or bad for newly industrializing countries? Are the most fundamental economic units individuals or classes? And so on. Yet today one gets the impression that all economists agree on just about everything of political importance. Yes, there are a few academic squabbles, but on general policy issues one hears over and over the phrase 'most competent economists agree that . . .' The trick of course is to deny the status of 'economist', or at least the adjective 'competent', to anyone who does not agree, thereby keeping the consensus intact. Non-economists are often dismissed as 'laymen' by the clerisy, and of course incompetents need not be taken seriously in any case. Consensus among the academic élite remains unchallenged by the rabble. Of course serious scholars cannot waste time refuting every crazy idea put forward by every idiot capable of writing a sentence. But good judgement requires much more openness than we have at present. Consensus has been taken as the hallmark of the scientific maturity of a discipline, and economists, in their eagerness to gain the prestige of a mature science, have taken the short cut of imposing consensus prematurely. From their point of view this collection of criticisms and reviews will be seen as a step backward – a move against consensus. But if we are going in the wrong direction a step backward is not a bad thing.

Finally, a word about the organization of the book. I have grouped the reviews and essays into seven subject areas and provided each with a short introduction, so that each section can be read more or less independently by readers with focused interests. It is probably too much to hope for, but I confess a special affection for anyone who reads this book from cover to cover in sequence.

Note
1.   See Juan Martinez-Alier, *Ecological Economics*, Basil Blackwell, Oxford, 1987.

I On the roots of error in growth economics

Introduction

The first essay, 'Boundless bull', is an attempt to identify and criticize in a popular way the presuppositions of the growth economy as they are presented in the media with hypnotic frequency. I encountered the image of the boundless bull repeatedly while watching the Wimbledon tennis finals on TV some years ago. I can't even remember who was playing, but the boundless bull in the commercials lodged in my memory for ever. In today's world images enter our minds much more often and convincingly than arguments. One should try to subject images to critical reflection. Another approach is to counter offending images with other images, as done by the organization called 'Ad busters' that puts out anti-consumerist images, such as a picture of 'Joe Chemo', a camel with cigarette and sunglasses dying of cancer in a hospital bed. One has a right to fight fire with fire, but my personal hope is that reasoned argument still has a place, and that right and wrong will not ultimately be decided only by warring advertising images. Hence my attempt to 'deconstruct' the boundless bull.

The second essay is more recent and, at least in intent, more scholarly. It attempts to explain philosophically and historically the pre-analytic basis of growth economics. Also I take some analytical first steps toward introducing into macroeconomics the crucial concept of the optimum scale of the macroeconomy relative to the ecosystem, along with the related concept of uneconomic growth. What lies beyond economic growth is uneconomic growth, and that, in a nutshell, is why growth must not go on indefinitely. This article provides the general framework and arguments that tie the other parts of the book together.

1   Boundless bull*

If you want to know what is wrong with the American economy it is not enough to go to graduate school, read books and study statistical trends – you also have to watch TV. Not the Sunday morning talking-head shows or even documentaries, and especially not the network news, but the really serious stuff – the commercials. For instance, the most penetrating insight into the American economy by far is contained in the image of the bull that trots unimpeded through countless Merrill Lynch commercials.

One such ad opens with a bull trotting along a beach. He is a very powerful animal – nothing is likely to stop him. And since the beach is empty as far as the eye can see, there is nothing that could even slow him down. A chorus in the background intones: 'to . . . know . . . no . . . boundaries . . .'. The bull trots off into the sunset.

Abruptly the scene shifts. The bull is now trotting across a bridge that spans a deep gorge. There are no bicycles, cars or 18-wheel trucks on the bridge, so again the bull is alone in an empty and unobstructed world. The chasm, which might have proved a barrier to the bull, who after all is not a mountain goat, is conveniently spanned by an empty bridge.

Next the bull finds himself in a forest of giant redwoods, looking just a bit lost as he tramples the underbrush. The camera zooms up the trunk of a giant redwood whose top disappears into the shimmering sunlight. The chorus chirps on about a 'world with no boundaries'.

Finally we see the bull silhouetted against a burgundy sunset, standing in solitary majesty atop a mesa overlooking a great empty southwestern desert. The silhouette clearly outlines the animal's genitalia, making it obvious even to city slickers that this is a bull, not a cow. Fadeout. The bull cult of ancient Crete and the Indus Valley, in which the bull god symbolized the virile principle of generation and invincible force, is alive and well on Wall Street.

The message is clear: Merrill Lynch wants to put you into an individualistic, macho world without limits – the US economy. The bull, of course,

* Published in *Gannett Center Journal*, **4** (3), Summer 1990, pp. 113–18; also in Craig L. LaMay and Everette E. Dennis (eds), *Media and the Environment*, Island Press, 1991, pp. 149–55. The views presented here are those of the author and should in no way be attributed to the World Bank.

also symbolizes rising stock prices and unlimited optimism, which is ultimately based on this vision of an empty world where strong, solitary individuals have free reign. This vision is what is most fundamentally wrong with the American economy. In addition to TV commercials it can be found in politicians' speeches, in economic textbooks, and between the ears of most economists and business journalists.

No bigger lie can be imagined. The world is not empty; it is full! Even where it is empty of people it is full of other things. In California it is so full that people shoot each other because freeway space is scarce. A few years ago they were shooting each other because gasoline was scarce. Reducing the gasoline shortage just aggravated the space shortage on the freeways.

Many species are driven to extinction each year due to takeover of their 'empty' habitat. Indigenous peoples are relocated to make way for dams and highways through 'empty' jungles. The 'empty' atmosphere is dangerously full of carbon dioxide and pollutants that fall as acid rain.

Unlike Merrill Lynch's bull, most bulls do not trot freely along empty beaches. Most are castrated and live their short lives as steers imprisoned in crowded, stinking feed lots. Like the steers, we too live in a world of imploding fullness. The bonds of community, both moral and biophysical, are stretched, or rather compressed, to breaking point. We have a massive foreign trade deficit, a domestic federal deficit, unemployment, declining real wages and inflation. Large accumulated debts, both foreign and domestic, are being used to finance consumption, not investment. Foreign ownership of the US economy is increasing, and soon domestic control over national economic life will decrease.

Why does Merrill Lynch (and the media and academia and the politicians) regale us with this 'boundless bull'? Do they believe it? Why do they want you to believe it, or at least to be influenced by it at a subconscious level? Because what they are selling is growth, and growth requires empty space to grow into. Solitary bulls don't have to share the world with other creatures, and neither do you! Growth means that what you get from your bullish investments does not come at anyone else's expense. In a world with no boundaries the poor can get richer while the rich get richer even faster. Our politicians find the boundless bull cult irresistible.

The boundless bull of unlimited growth appears in economics text-books with less colourful imagery but greater precision. Economists abstract from natural resources because they do not consider them scarce, or because they think that they can be perfectly substituted by man-made capital. The natural world either puts no obstacles in the bull's path or, if an obstacle like the chasm appears, capital (the bridge) effectively removes it.

Economics textbooks also assume that wants are unlimited. Merrill Lynch's boundless bull is always on the move. What if, like Ferdinand, he were just to sit, smell the flowers, and be content with the world as it is without trampling it underfoot? That would not do. If you are selling continual growth then you have to sell continual, restless, trotting dissatisfaction with the world as it is, as well as the notion that it has no boundaries.

This pre-analytic vision colours the analysis even of good economists, and many people never get beyond the boundless bull scenario. Certainly the media have not. Would it be asking too much of the media to do what professional economists have failed to do? Probably so, but all disciplines badly need external critics, and in the universities disciplines do not criticize each other. Even philosophy, which historically was the critic of the separate disciplines, has abdicated that role. Who is left? Economist Joan Robinson put it well many years ago when she noted that economists have run off to hide in thickets of algebra and left the really serious problems of economic policy to be handled by journalists. Is it to the media that we must turn for disciplinary criticism, for new analytic thinking about the economy? The thought does not inspire confidence. But in the land of the blind the one-eyed man is king. If journalists are to criticize the disciplinary orthodoxy of economic growth, they will need both the energy provided by moral outrage and the clarity of thought provided by some basic analytic distinctions.

Moral outrage should result from the dawning realization that we are destroying the capacity of the earth to support life and counting it as progress, or at best as the inevitable cost of progress. 'Progress' evidently means converting as much as possible of Creation into ourselves and our furniture. 'Ourselves' means, concretely, the unjust combination of overpopulated slums and overconsuming suburbs. Since we do not have the courage to face up to sharing and population control as the solution to injustice, we pretend that further growth will make the poor better off instead of simply making the rich richer. The wholesale extinctions of other species, and some primitive cultures within our own species, are not reckoned as costs. The intrinsic value of other species, their own capacity to enjoy life, is not admitted at all in economics, and their instrumental value as providers of ecological life-support services to humans is only dimly perceived. Costs and benefits to future humans are routinely discounted at 10 per cent, meaning that each dollar of cost or benefit 50 years in the future is valued at less than a penny today.

But just getting angry is not sufficient. Doing something requires clear thinking, and clear thinking requires calling different things by different names. The most important analytic distinction comes straight from the dictionary definitions of growth and development. 'To grow' means to increase in size by the accretion or assimilation of material. 'Growth' therefore means a quantitative increase in the scale of the physical dimensions of the economy. 'To develop' means to expand or realize the potentialities of; to bring gradually to a fuller, greater or better state. 'Development' therefore means the qualitative improvement in the structure, design and composition of the physical stocks of wealth that results from greater knowledge, both of technique and of purpose. A growing economy is getting bigger; a developing economy is getting better. An economy can therefore develop without growing, or grow without developing. A steady-state economy is one that does not grow, but is free to develop. It is not static – births replace deaths and production replaces depreciation, so that stocks of wealth and people are continually renewed and even improved, although neither is growing. Consider a steady-state library. Its stock of books is constant but not static. As a book becomes worn out or obsolete it is replaced by a new or better one. The quality of the library improves, but its physical stock of books does not grow. The library develops without growing. Likewise the economy's physical stock of people and artefacts can develop without growing.

The advantage of defining growth in terms of change in physical scale of the economy is that it forces us to think about the effects of a change in scale and directs attention to the concept of an ecologically sustainable scale, or perhaps even of an optimal scale. The scale of the economy is the product of population times per capita resource use – that is, the total flow of resources – a flow that might conceivably be ecologically unsustainable, especially in a finite world that is not empty.

The notion of an optimal scale for an activity is the very heart of microeconomics. For every activity, be it eating ice cream or making shoes, there is a cost function and a benefit function, and the rule is to increase the scale of the activity up to the point where rising marginal cost equals falling marginal benefit – that is, to where the desire for another ice cream is equal to the desire to keep the money for something else, or the extra cost of making another pair of shoes is just equal to the extra revenue from selling the shoes. Yet for the macro level, the aggregate of all microeconomic activities (shoe making, ice cream eating and everything else), there is no concept of an optimal scale. The notion that the macroeconomy could become too large relative to the ecosystem is simply absent from macroeconomic theory. The macro-economy is supposed to grow for ever. Since GNP adds costs and benefits together instead of comparing them at the margin, we have no macro-level accounting by which an optimal scale could be identified. Beyond a certain scale growth begins to destroy more values than it creates – economic growth gives way to an era of anti-economic growth. But GNP keeps rising, giving us no clue as to whether we have passed that critical point!

The apt image for the US economy, then, is not the boundless bull on the empty beach, but the proverbial bull in the china shop. The bound-less bull is too big and clumsy relative to its delicate environment. Why must it keep growing when it is already destroying more than its extra mass is worth?

Because: (1) We fail to distinguish growth from development, and we classify all scale expansion as 'economic growth' without even recog-nizing the possibility of 'anti-economic growth' – that is, growth that costs us more than it is worth at the margin; (2) we refuse to fight poverty by redistribution and sharing, or by controlling our own numbers, leaving 'economic' growth as the only acceptable cure for poverty. But once we are beyond the optimal scale and growth makes us poorer rather than richer, even that reason becomes absurd. Sharing, population control and true qualitative development are difficult. They are also collective virtues that for the most part cannot be attained by individual action and that do not easily give rise to increased opportuni-ties for private profit. The boundless bull is much easier to sell, and profitable at least to some while the illusion lasts. But further growth has become destructive of community, the environment and the common good. If the media could help economists and politicians to see that, or at least to entertain the possibility that such a thing might be true, they would have rendered a service far greater than all the reporting of statistics on GNP growth, Dow Jones indexes and junk bond prices from now until the end of time.

2 Uneconomic growth: in theory, in fact, in history, and in relation to globalization

That which seems to be wealth may in verity be only the gilded index of far-reaching ruin . . .

John Ruskin, *Unto this Last*, 1862

1. Uneconomic growth in theory

Growth in GNP is so favoured by economists that they call it 'economic' growth, thus ruling out by terminological baptism the very possibility of 'uneconomic' growth in GNP. But can growth in GNP in fact be uneconomic? Before answering this macroeconomic question, let us consider the same question in the perspective of microeconomics – can growth in a microeconomic activity (firm production or household consumption) be uneconomic? Of course it can. Indeed, all of microeconomics is simply a variation on the theme of seeking the optimal scale or extent of each micro activity – the point where increasing marginal cost equals declining marginal benefit, and beyond which further growth in the activity would be uneconomic because it would increase costs more than benefits. Quite aptly, the MB = MC condition is sometimes called the 'when-to-stop rule'.

But when we move to macroeconomics we no longer hear anything about optimal scale, nor about marginal costs and benefits; nor is there anything like a 'when-to-stop rule'. Instead of separate accounts of costs and benefits compared at the margin, we have just one account, GNP, that conflates cost and benefits into the single category of 'economic activity'. The faith is that activity overwhelmingly reflects benefits. There is no macroeconomic analogue of costs of activity to balance against and hold in check the growth of 'activity', identified with benefits, and measured by GNP. Unique among economic magnitudes, GNP is supposed to grow for ever.[1] But of course there really are costs incurred by GNP growth, even if they are not usually measured. There are costs of depletion, pollution, disruption of ecological life-support services, sacrifice of leisure time, disutility of some kinds of labour, destruction of community in the interests of capital mobility, takeover of habitat of other species, and running down a critical part of the inheritance of future generations. We not only fail to measure these costs, but

8

frequently we implicitly count them as benefits, as when we include the costs of cleaning up pollution as a part of GNP, and when we fail to deduct for depreciation of renewable natural capital (productive capacity), and liquidation of non-renewable natural capital (inventories).

There is no *a priori* reason why at the margin the costs of growth in GNP could not be greater than the benefits. In fact economic theory would lead us to expect that to happen eventually. The law of diminishing marginal utility of income tells us that we satisfy our most pressing wants first, and that each additional unit of income is dedicated to the satisfaction of a less pressing want. So the marginal benefit of growth declines. Similarly, the law of increasing marginal costs tells us that we first make use of the most productive and accessible factors of production – the most fertile land, the most concentrated and available mineral deposits, the best workers – and only use the less productive factors as growth makes it necessary. Consequently, marginal costs increase with growth. When rising marginal costs equal falling marginal benefits then we are at the optimal level of GNP, and further growth would be uneconomic – would increase costs more than it increased benefits. Why is this simple extension of the basic logic of microeconomics treated as inconceivable in the domain of macroeconomics?[2] Mainly because microeconomics deals with the part, and expansion of a part is limited by the opportunity cost inflicted on the rest of the whole by the growth of the part under study. Macroeconomics deals with the whole, and the growth of the whole does not inflict an opportunity cost, because there is no 'rest of the whole' to suffer the cost. Ecological economists have pointed out that the macroeconomy is not the relevant whole, but is itself a subsystem, a part of the ecosystem, the larger economy of nature.

These ideas are represented in Figures 2.1 and 2.2. Figure 2.1 shows the pre-analytic vision of ecological economics – the economy as subsystem of a larger ecosystem that is finite, non-growing, and materially closed. The ecosystem is open with respect to a flow of solar energy, but that flow is itself finite and non-growing. There is an 'empty-world' and a 'full-world' version of this basic vision, reflecting the fact that people who share the same paradigm can have differing senses of urgency based on different interpretations of 'the facts'. Both will agree, however, that the goal is an optimal scale of the economy relative to the ecosystem. The optimal scale is that for which welfare is greatest.

We have two general sources of welfare: services of man-made capital and services of natural capital, as represented in Figure 2.1. As the economy grows, natural capital is transformed into man-made capital.

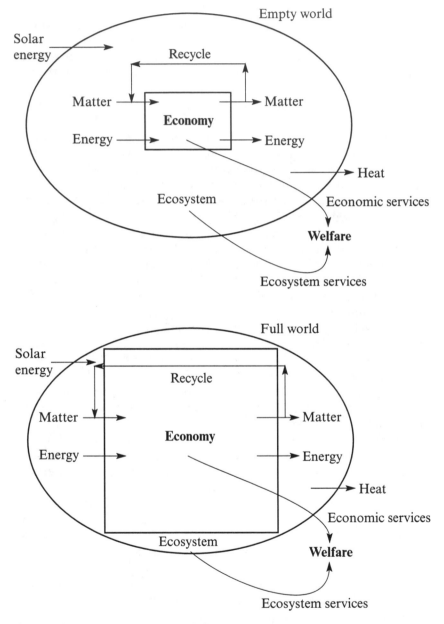

Figure 2.1   A 'macro' view of the macroeconomy

More man-made capital results in a greater flow of services from that source. Reduced natural capital results in a smaller flow of services from that source. Moreover, as growth of the economy continues, the services from the economy grow at a decreasing rate. As rational beings we satisfy our most pressing wants first – hence the law of diminishing marginal utility. As the economy encroaches more and more on the ecosystem we must give up some ecosystem services. As rational beings we will presumably sequence our encroachments so that we sacrifice the least important ecosystem services first. This is the best case, the goal. In actuality we fall short of it because we do not understand very well how the ecosystem works, and have only recently begun to think of it as scarce. But the consequence of such rational sequencing is a version of the law of increasing marginal cost – for each further unit of economic expansion we must give up a more important ecosystem service. Costs increase at an increasing rate.

This first step in analysis of the pre-analytic vision can be expressed in a diagram (Figure 2.2) whose basic logic goes back to William Stanley Jevons (1871) and his analysis of labour supply in terms of balancing the marginal utility of wages with the marginal disutility of labour. In Figure 2.2 the *MU* curve reflects the diminishing marginal utility of additions to the stock of man-made capital. The *MDU* curve reflects the increasing marginal cost of growth (sacrificed natural capital services, disutility of labour, disruption of community), as more natural capital is transformed into man-made capital. The optimal scale of the macro-economy (economic limit to growth) is at point *b*, where *MU* = *MDU*, or where *ab* = *bc*, and net positive utility is a maximum.

Two further limits are noted: point *e*, where *MU* = 0 and further growth is futile even with zero cost; and point *d*, where an ecological catastrophe is provoked, driving *MDU* to infinity. These 'outer limits' need not occur in the order depicted. Figure 2.2 shows that growth out to point *b* is literally economic growth (benefiting us more than it costs), while growth beyond point *b* is literally uneconomic growth (costing us more than it benefits). Beyond point *b*, GNP, 'that which seems to be wealth', does indeed become 'a gilded index of far-reaching ruin.'

The concepts of optimal scale and uneconomic growth have a universal logic – they apply to the macroeconomy just as much as to microeconomic units. How did we come to forget this in macroeconomics? How did we come to ignore the existence of the *MDU* curve and the issue of optimal scale of the macroeconomy? I will suggest two possibilities: one is the 'empty-world' vision' that recognizes the logical coherence of the concept of uneconomic growth, but claims that we are not yet at that point – *MU* is still very large, and *MDU* is still

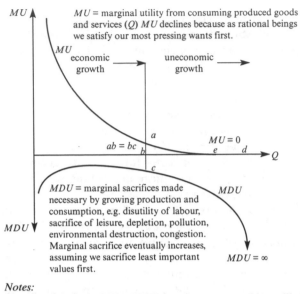

Notes:
b = economic limit; $MU = MDU$ (maximum net positive utility);
e = futility limit; $MU = 0$ (consumer satiation);
d = catastrophe limit; $MDU = \infty$ (ecological disaster)

Figure 2.2 Jevonian view of limits to growth of macroeconomy

negligible. Here we can discuss the factual evidence, as will be done in the next section.

The other possibility for explaining the total neglect of the costs of growth is a paradigm difference: the economy is simply not seen as a subsystem of the ecosystem, but rather the reverse – the ecosystem is a subsystem of the economy (Figure 2.3). The ecosystem is merely the extractive and waste disposal sector of the economy. Even if these services become scarce, growth can continue for ever since technology allows us to 'grow around' the ecosystem sector by substitution of man-made for natural capital, following the dictates of market prices – if and when prices of natural capital rise. Nature is really nothing but a supplier of indestructible building blocks which are substitutable and superabundant. The only limit to growth is technology, and there is, supposedly, no limit to technology, *ergo* no limit to economic growth. Therefore the very notion of 'uneconomic growth' makes no sense in that paradigm. Since the economy is the whole, the growth of the economy is not at the expense of anything else – there is no opportunity cost to growth. On the contrary, growth enlarges the total to be shared by the different sectors or subsystems. Growth does not increase the scarcity of anything; rather it diminishes the scarcity of everything! How can one possibly oppose growth? Growth for ever, or a steady state at optimal scale? Each is logical within its own pre-analytic vision, and absurd from the viewpoint of the other. We will return in Section 3 to the paradigm issue, but first let us consider some evidence in favour of the full-world version of the pre-analytic vision of ecological economics.

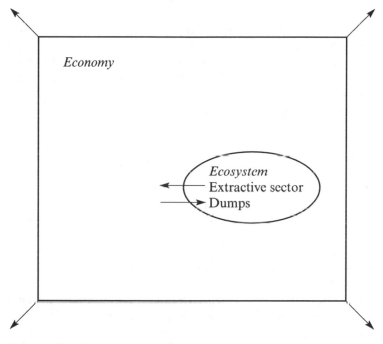

Figure 2.3 Ecosystem as subsystem of macroeconomy

2. Uneconomic growth in fact

As noted above, one might accept the theoretical possibility of uneconomic growth, but argue that it is irrelevant for practical purposes since, it could be alleged, we are nowhere near the optimal scale. We are thought to be far to the left of point *b* in Figure 2.2 – where the benefits of growth are still enormous and the costs still trivial at the margin. Economists all agree that GNP was not designed to be a measure of welfare, but only of activity. Nevertheless they assume that welfare is positively correlated with activity, so that increasing GNP will increase welfare, even if not on a one-for-one basis. This is equivalent to believing that the marginal benefit of GNP growth is greater than the marginal cost. This belief can be put to an empirical test. The results turn out not to support the belief.

Evidence for doubting the positive correlation between GNP and welfare in the USA is taken from from two sources.

First Nordhaus and Tobin[3] asked, 'Is Growth Obsolete?' as a measure of welfare, hence as a proper guiding objective of policy. To answer their question they developed a direct index of welfare, called Measured Economic Welfare (MEW) and tested its correlation with GNP over the period 1929–65. They found that, for the period as a whole, GNP and MEW were indeed positively correlated – for every six units of increase in GNP there was, on average, a four-unit increase in MEW. Economists breathed a sigh of relief, forgot about MEW, and concentrated again on GNP. Although GNP was not designed as a measure of welfare, it was and still is thought to be sufficiently well correlated with welfare to serve as a practical guide for policy.

Some twenty years later John Cobb, Clifford Cobb and I revisited the issue and began development of our Index of Sustainable Economic Welfare (ISEW) with a review of the Nordhaus and Tobin MEW. We discovered that if one takes only the latter half of their time series (that is, the 18 years from 1947 to 1965), the positive correlation between GNP and MEW *falls* dramatically. In this most recent period – surely the more relevant for projections into the future – a six-unit increase in GNP yielded on average only a one-unit increase in MEW. This suggests that GNP growth at this stage of US history may be a quite inefficient way of improving economic welfare – certainly less efficient than in the past.

The ISEW[4] was then developed to replace MEW, since the latter omitted any correction for environmental costs, did not correct for distributional changes, and included leisure which both dominated the MEW and introduced many arbitrary valuation decisions. The ISEW, like the MEW, though less so, was positively correlated with GNP up to a point (around 1980) beyond which the correlation turned slightly negative. Neither the MEW nor the ISEW considered the effect of individual country GNP growth on the *global* environment, and consequently on welfare of citizens of other countries. Neither was there any deduction for legal harmful products, such as tobacco or alcohol, nor illegal harmful products such as drugs. No deduction was made for diminishing marginal utility of income resulting from growth over time (although there was a distributional correction for the higher marginal utility of income to the poor). Such considerations would further push the correlation between GNP and welfare toward the negative. Also, GNP, MEW and ISEW all begin with personal consumption. Since all three measures have in common their largest single category, there is a significant autocorrelation bias, which makes the poor correlations between GNP and the two welfare measures all the more impressive.

Measures of welfare are difficult and subject to many arbitrary judgements, so sweeping conclusions should be resisted. However, it seems fair to say that for the USA since 1947, the empirical evidence that GNP growth has increased welfare is weak, and since 1980 probably non-existent. Consequently, any impact on welfare via policies that increase GNP growth would also be weak or non-existent. In other words, the 'great benefit', for which we are urged to sacrifice the environment, community standards and industrial peace, appears, on closer inspection, likely not even to exist.[5]

3. Uneconomic growth in two paradigms

Within the standard neoclassical paradigm uneconomic growth sounds like an oxymoron, or at least an anomalous category. You will not find the concept in any macroeconomics textbook. But within the paradigm of ecological economics it is an obvious possibility. Let us consider why in each case.

Neoclassical paradigm

The paradigm or pre-analytic vision of standard neoclassical economics, as noted earlier and depicted in Figure 2.3, is that the economy is the total system, and that nature, to the extent that it is considered at all, is a sector of the economy – for example the extractive sector (mines, wells, forests, fisheries, agriculture, including dumps). Nature is not seen as an envelope containing, provisioning and sustaining the economy, but as one sector of the economy similar to other sectors. If the products or services of the extractive sector should become scarce, the economy will 'grow around' that particular scarcity by substituting the products of other sectors. If the substitution is difficult, new technologies, it is argued, will be invented to make it easy.

The unimportance of nature is evidenced, in this view, by the falling relative prices of extractive products generally, and by the declining share of the extractive sector in total GNP. Beyond the initial provision of indestructible building blocks, nature is simply not important to the economy in the view of neoclassical economics.

That the above is a fair description of the neoclassical paradigm is attested by the elementary 'principles of economics' textbooks, all of which present the shared pre-analytic vision in their initial pages. This, of course, is the famous circular flow diagram, depicting the economy as a circular flow of exchange value between firms and households – as an isolated system in which nothing enters from outside nor exits to the outside. There is no 'outside', no environment. The economic animal has neither mouth nor anus – only a closed-loop circular gut – the biological version of a perpetual motion machine! Further confirmation is found by searching the indexes of macroeconomics textbooks for any entries such as 'environment', 'nature', 'depletion', or 'pollution'. The absence of such entries is nearly complete. As if to reaffirm the unimportance of nature, the advanced textbook chapters on growth theory are based on a neoclassical production function in which production is represented as a function of labour and capital only, with resources totally absent!

A personal experience confirmed to me even more forcefully just how deeply ingrained this pre-analytic vision really is. I think it is worth taking the time to recount this experience, which had to do with the evolution of the World Bank's 1992 *World Development Report: Development and the Environment*.

An early draft of the 1992 *WDR* had a diagram entitled 'The relationship between the economy and the environment'. It consisted of a square labelled 'economy', with an arrow coming in labelled 'inputs' and an arrow going out labelled 'outputs' – nothing more. I worked in the Environment Department of the World Bank at that time, and was asked to review and comment on the draft. I suggested that the picture was a good idea, but that it failed to show the environment, and that it would help to have a larger box containing the one depicted, and that the large box (or circle, perhaps) would represent the environment. Then the relation between the environment and the economy would be clear – specifically that the economy is a subsystem of the environment and depends on the environment both as a source of raw material inputs and as a sink for waste outputs. The text accompanying the diagram should explain that the environment physically contains and sustains the economy by regenerating the low-entropy inputs that it requires, and by absorbing the high-entropy wastes that it cannot avoid generating, as well as by supplying other systemic ecological services. Environmentally sustainable development could then be defined as development which does not destroy these natural support functions.

The second draft had the same diagram, but with an unlabelled box drawn around the economy, like a picture frame, with no change in the text. I commented that, while this was a step forward, the larger box really had to be labelled 'environment' or else it was merely decorative, and that the text had to explain that the economy was related to the environment in the ways just described.

The third draft omitted the diagram altogether. There was no further effort to draw a picture of the relation between the economy and the environment. Why was it so hard to draw such a simple picture?

By coincidence a few months later the Chief Economist of the World Bank, under whom the 1992 *WDR* was being written, happened to be on a review panel at the Smithsonian Institution discussing the book *Beyond the Limits* (Donella Meadows et al.). In that book there was a diagram showing the relation of the economy to the ecosystem as subsystem to total system, identical to what I had suggested (and to Figure 2.1). In the question-and-answer time I asked the Chief Economist if, looking at that diagram, he felt that the issue of the physical size of the economic subsystem relative to the total ecosystem was important, and if he thought economists should be asking the question, 'What is the optimal scale of the macroeconomy relative to the environment that supports it?' His reply was short and definite: 'That's not the right way to look at it', he said.

Reflecting on these two experiences has strengthened my belief that the difference truly lies in our 'pre-analytic vision' – the way we look at it. My pre-analytic vision of the economy as subsystem leads immediately to the questions: How big *is* the subsystem relative to the total system? How big *can it be* without disrupting the functioning of the total system? How big *should it be* – what is its optimal scale beyond which further growth in scale would be uneconomic? The Chief Economist had no intention of being sucked into these subversive questions – that is not the right way to look at it, and any questions arising from that way of looking at it are simply not the right questions.

That attitude sounds rather unreasonable and peremptory, but in a way that had also been my response to the diagram in the first draft of *Development and the Environment*, showing the economy receiving raw material inputs from nowhere and exporting waste outputs to nowhere. 'That is not the right way to look at it', I said, and any questions arising from that picture, for example how to make the economy grow faster by speeding up throughput from an infinite source to an infinite sink, were not the right questions. Unless one has in mind the pre-analytic vision of the economy as subsystem, the whole idea of sustainable development – of an economic subsystem being sustained by a larger ecosystem whose carrying capacity it must respect – makes no sense whatsoever. It was not surprising therefore that the 1992 *WDR* was incoherent on the subject of sustainable development, placing it in solitary confinement in a half-page box where it was implicitly defined as nothing other than 'good development policy'. It is the pre-analytic vision of the economy as a box floating in infinite space that allows people to speak of 'sustainable *growth*' (quantitative expansion) as opposed to 'sustainable *development*' (qualitative improvement). The former term is self-contradictory to those who see the economy as a subsystem of a finite and non-growing ecosystem. The difference could not be more fundamental, more elementary, or more irreconcilable.

Ecological economics paradigm

This story of course leads to a consideration of the alternative paradigm, that of ecological economics within which uneconomic growth is an obvious concept. The big difference is to see the economy as a subsystem of the natural ecosystem.

The neoclassical 'evidence' for the unimportance of nature (falling relative price of many natural resources, and small share of the extractive sector in GNP) is seen quite differently in the ecological economics paradigm. In an era of rapid extraction of resources their short-run supply will of course be high and their market price consequently will be low. Low resources prices are not evidence of non-scarcity and unimportance, but rather a consequence of rapid drawdown, leading to increasing technological dependence on a large throughput of cheap resources. As for the neoclassical claim that the small percentage of GNP arising from the extractive sector indicates its unimportance, one might as well claim that a building's foundation is unimportant because it represents only 5 per cent of the height of the skyscraper erected above it. GNP is the sum of value *added* by labour and capital. But added to what? Resources are *that to which value is added* – the base or foundation upon which the skyscraper of added value is resting. A foundation's importance does not diminish with the growth of the structure that it supports! Nevertheless, economists habitually argue the contrary. They say, for example, that we need not worry about global warming because the only climate-sensitive sector of the economy is agriculture, and agriculture accounts for only 3 per cent of GNP. These economists evidently don't need to eat – perhaps they come equipped with a closed-loop gut similar to what they assume in their circular flow diagram! They also need remedial reflection on the diamonds–water paradox.

If GNP growth resulted only from increments in value added to a non-growing resource throughput, then it would probably remain *economic* growth for much longer. Such a process of qualitative improvement without quantitative increase beyond environmental capacity is what I have elsewhere[6] termed 'development without growth', and suggested as a definition of 'sustainable development'. But that is not yet what happens in today's world. According to the World Resources Institute et al., per capita resource requirement rose, albeit slowly, over the period 1975–93 in Germany, Japan and The Netherlands. It also rose in the USA if one does not count reductions in soil erosion. Population growth in these countries is low, but not zero, giving a further boost to total throughput growth. Since current levels of resource throughput in these countries range from 45 to 85 thousand kilograms per person per year, a level already causing severe environmental degradation, it seems a bit premature to herald the advent of the 'dematerialized economy'.[7]

What happens, according to ecological economics, is that the economy grows by transforming its environment (natural capital) into itself (man-made capital). The optimal extent of this physical transformation (optimal scale of the economy) occurs, as previously shown, when the marginal cost of natural capital reduction is equal to the marginal benefit of man-made capital increase. This process of transformation takes place within a total environment that is finite, non-growing, and materially closed. There is a throughput of solar energy which powers biogeochemical cycles, but that energy throughput is also finite and non-growing. As the economic subsystem grows it becomes a larger part of the total system, and therefore must conform itself more to the limits of the total system – finitude, non-growth and entropy. Its growth is ultimately limited by the size of the total system of which it is a part, even under neoclassical assumptions of easy substitution of man-made for natural capital.

But if man-made and natural capital are complements rather than substitutes, as ecological economics claims, then expansion of the economic subsystem would be much more stringently limited. There would be no point in expanding man-made capital beyond the capacity of remaining natural capital to complement it. The fish catch used to be limited by number of fishing boats (man-made capital) but is now limited by the remaining populations of fish in the sea (natural capital). What good are more fishing boats when the fish population has become the limiting factor?

When factors are complements the one in short supply is *limiting*. If factors are substitutes then there cannot be a limiting factor. Economic logic says that we should focus attention on the limiting factor by: (a) maximizing its productivity in the short run; and (b) investing in its increase in the long run. This is a *major* implication for economic policy – economize on and invest in natural capital. Economic logic stays the same, but the identity of the limiting factor has gradually changed from man-made to natural capital, for example from fishing boats to remaining fish in the sea; from sawmills to remaining forests; from irrigation systems to aquifers or rivers; from oil-well drilling rigs to pools of petroleum in the ground; from engines that burn fossil fuel to the atmosphere's capacity to absorb CO_2, and so on.

Viewed from the perspective of ecological economics, even the usual neoclassical assumption of easy substitution of man-made for natural capital (and consequent neglect of limiting-factor phenomena) provides no argument for continual growth, even though it relaxes the tightest constraint on present growth. If man-made capital substitutes for natural capital, then natural capital substitutes for man-made capital. Substitution is reversible. If our original endowment of natural capital was a good substitute for man-made capital, then why, historically, did we go to the trouble of transforming so much natural capital into man-made capital? Neoclassical believers in easy substitution have no good answer. Nor do they have a very good answer to the question: How can you make more capital without using more resources? The problem does not arise for ecological economists because they affirm from the beginning that natural and man-made capital are basically complements and only marginally substitutes.

The optimal scale of the economy is smaller, the greater (a) the degree of complementarity between natural and man-made capital; (b) our desire for direct experience of nature; and (c) our estimate of both the intrinsic and instrumental value of other species. The smaller the optimal scale of the economy, the sooner its physical growth becomes uneconomic.

4. From permitting growth, to mandating growth, to limiting growth

The neoclassical paradigm permits growth for ever but does not really mandate it. Historically, what pushed the growth-forever ideology was not neoclassical logic, but rather the practical answer given to the problems addressed by Malthus (overpopulation), Marx (unjust distribution), and Keynes (involuntary unemployment). Growth was the common answer to all three problems.

Overpopulation would be cured by the demographic transition. When GNP per capita reaches a certain level, children become too expensive in terms of other goods foregone and the birth rate automatically falls. Economic growth is the best contraceptive, as the slogan goes. Whether the product of increased per capita consumption times the decreased birth rate of 'capitas' results in increasing total consumption beyond optimal scale remains an unasked question. More concretely, is it necessary for Indian per capita consumption to rise to the Swedish level for

Indian fertility to fall to the Swedish level, and if so what happens to the Indian ecosystem as a result of that level of total consumption?

Unjust distribution of wealth between classes would be rendered tolerable by growth, the rising tide that lifts all boats, to recall another slogan. Yet growth has in fact increased inequality both within and among nations. To make matters worse, even the metaphor is wrong, since a rising tide in one part of the world implies an ebbing tide somewhere else.

Unemployment would yield to increasing aggregate demand which merely required that investment be stimulated, which of course implies growth. How long can we continue to avoid unemployment by growth? Must we grow beyond optimal scale in persuit of full employment? Another unasked question.

Continuing this time-honoured tradition, the World Bank's 1992 *WDR* argued that more growth was also the automatic solution to the environmental problem. A so-called 'environmental Kuznets curve' was discovered, which was taken to reveal an inverted U-shaped relation between GNP and a number of environmental pollutants. Consequently, one must must persevere in growth because even though it is bad for the environment initially, it will later be good for the environment once we pass the hump of the inverted U.

But of course the assumption in all cases is that growth is economic, that it is making us richer rather than poorer. But now growth is becoming uneconomic. Uneconomic growth will not sustain the demographic transition and cure overpopulation. Neither will it help redress unjust distribution, nor cure unemployment. Nor will it provide extra wealth to be devoted to environmental repair and clean-up. Indirect growth-based solutions to the big problems no longer work.

We now need more direct and radical solutions to the problems of Malthus, Marx and Keynes: population control to deal with overpopulation; redistribution to deal with excessive inequality; and measures such as a public employer of last resort, and ecological tax reform to raise resource prices relative to labour. These must be national policies. It is utopian (or dystopian) to think of them being carried out by a world authority. Many nations have made progress in controlling their population growth, in limiting domestic income inequality, in reducing unemployment. They have also improved resource productivity by internalizing environmental and social costs into prices. But nations' efforts in this regard are undercut by the ideology of globalization – a last-gasp attempt to re-establish the conditions of the empty-world economy by growing into the economic and ecological space of other countries, and into the remaining global commons.

5. Globalization as stimulus to uneconomic growth

Global economic integration by free trade and free capital mobility effectively erases the policy significance of national boundaries, turning the federated community of nations into a cosmopolitan non-community of globalized individuals. Some of these 'individuals' are giant transnational corporations, but are treated legally as fictitious individuals. Nations can no longer internalize environmental and social costs in the interests of resource efficiency and social justice, because capital is free to produce elsewhere and still sell its product in the market whose social controls it just escaped. In like manner, capital escapes higher wages and taxes of any kind, in particular taxes aimed at redistributive policies that redress excessive inequality and poverty.

Just as it is hard to imagine a country internalizing its external costs when forced to trade freely with countries that do not, so too is it hard to imagine any country continuing to limit its birth rate when the results of overpopulation in other countries spill over into it. Whether capital moves to overpopulated low-wage countries, or poor workers move to the high-wage country, the result is the same – a competitive bidding down of wages to the detriment of countries that have followed a high-wage policy by limiting their numbers and more equally distributing their wealth. The labouring class in the low-wage country gains in terms of number employed, though not usually in terms of increased wages because of the virtually unlimited supply of cheap labour resulting from past and present demographic growth. The capitalist class in the high-wage country gains from lower wage costs at home as well as abroad.

The big losers are workers in the (formerly) high-wage countries. Indeed, with low wages now a competitive advantage in attracting capital, we might expect policies aimed at increasing the supply of labour in previously high-wage countries. Already the *Wall Street Journal* calls for easy immigration into the USA. Before long someone will probably advocate higher birth rates for the labouring class in high-wage countries as a solution for alleged 'labour shortages'. Furthermore, with falling real wages and disappearing social security, it is possible that we might even have a reversion to larger working-class families in search of security and community – a reverse demographic transition.

Under globalization, each country seeks to overcome national limits to its growth by growing into international ecological and economic space, as well as into the remaining global commons. Globalization operates by standards-lowering competition to bid down wages, to externalize environmental costs, and reduce social overhead charges for welfare, education and other public goods. It is far worse than an unrealistic global dream – it actively undercuts the ability of nations to continue to deal with their own problems of overpopulation, unjust distribution, unemployment and external costs. It converts many relatively tractable national problems into a single intractable global problem.

Globalization via export-led growth is the new philosopher's stone of the IMF–IBRD–WTO alchemists.[8] Nations can all turn their lead into gold by free trade. With the revival of alchemy comes a return to the logic of mercantilism: wealth is gold, and the way for countries without mines to get gold is to export more goods than they import, and receive payment for the difference in gold – the alchemy of trade. The way to export more than you import is to reduce wages, and to externalize social and environmental costs, because that keeps prices of your exports competitive. Low wages also prevent your labouring-class majority from importing and thereby dissipating the trade surplus. The way to keep wages low is to have an oversupply of labour. An oversupply of labour can be attained by easy immigration and high birth rates among the working class. Globalization requires, therefore, that for a nation to be rich, the working-class majority of its citizens must be poor, increase in number, and live in a deteriorating environment. Behind these absurdities is the further contradiction that under globalization it no longer makes sense to speak of 'nations' (only corporations); nor of 'citizens' (only employees).

Truly, globalization is accelerating the shift to an era of uneconomic growth, a time when, as John Ruskin foresaw,

That which seems to be wealth may in verity be only the gilded index of far-reaching ruin . . .

Notes

1. Although macroeconomists see no limits on the *size* of GNP, they have recognized a limit on its *rate of growth* in the form of inflation that results as the economy approaches full employment. This is seen more as an institutional limit than a biophysical one.

2. Of course if wants and technology change, as surely they do, then the optimal level of GNP will change. But there would then be another optimum beyond which growth would again be uneconomic. It is gratuitous to assume that changes in wants and technology will always be of a kind that results in a larger optimal GNP. The growth-forever paradigm has been saved in practice by: increasing focus on insatiable relative wants to the neglect of satiable absolute wants, aggressive advertising, increasing debt, and falling monetary costs of production attained by externalization of the real costs of more powerful and dangerous technologies.

3. William Nordhaus and James Tobin, 'Is Growth Obsolete?', in *Economic Growth*, National Bureau of Economic Research, New York, Columbia University Press, 1972.

4. For critical discussion and the latest revision of the ISEW, see Clifford W. Cobb and John B. Cobb, Jr et al., *The Green National Product*, University Press of America, New York, 1994. For a presentation of the ISEW see Appendix of H. Daly and J.

Cobb, *For the Common Good*, Boston: Beacon Press, 1989; second edition 1994. See also Clifford W. Cobb, et al., 'If the GDP is Up, Why is America Down?', *Atlantic Monthly*, October 1995.

5. For further evidence from other countries, see Manfred Max-Neef, 'Economic Growth and Quality of Life: A Threshold Hypothesis', *Ecological Economics*, **15** (1995), pp. 115–18.

6. See H. Daly, *Beyond Growth: The Economics of Sustainable Development*, Boston, MA: Beacon Press, 1966.

7. World Resources Institute et al., *Natural Resource Flows: The Material Basis of Industrial Economies*, Washington, DC, April 1997.

8. To these acronyms we may soon have to add MAI (Multilateral Agreement on Investment), a proposal currently being pushed in the OECD as a first step toward world agreement. This agreement would impose *de jure* what is now being achieved *de facto* by standards-lowering competition to attract mobile capital – namely the erasure of any distinction between national and foreign investment.

II On some specific errors in growth economics

Introduction

The review of Julian Simon is probably the most polemical part of this collection. Julian Simon died in 1998 and even his obituary in the *Washington Post* continued his battle for more economic growth and population growth, without limits. I have to admire his fighting spirit, even while finding his ideas to be illusory. I also think that Julian was badly used by standard economists. They never came to his defence in debates because they rightly considered his views hard to defend – and yet he was simply carrying the standard premises to their logical conclusion. Standard economists lacked the courage either to affirm the full consequences of their premises, or to re-examine those premises in the light of their absurd implications. Julian, at least, was logically consistent on that score, undeterred by the absurd implications that gave pause to the standard economists.

Free market environmentalism as expounded by Anderson and Leal also combines the virtue of logical adherence to basic premises with an unwillingness to re-examine those premises even when they lead to the advocacy of such dubious policies as genetically branding privately owned whales and monitoring them by satellite as 'cattle' on the common range of the oceans.

Wilfred Beckerman has long been an articulate defender of standard economics, and is worth reading because he now and then teaches us something, even though he remains faithful to the basic premises, although with less abandon than Julian Simon. Also, Beckerman was listened to quite seriously as an adviser to the World Bank.

I include here my farewell lecture to the World Bank because it is very relevant to the theories here discussed, even though it arose out of a more practical context – six years at the World Bank trying to push for environmental policies and against globalization by export-led growth and natural capital drawdown. However, I do not think it is possible to reform the World Bank without a major reform of academic economics. The World Bank is like the Church – trying to do good in the world. But its clergy all graduated from bad seminaries that taught idolatrous theology. The World Bank is the world's largest and most generous employer of economists, most of whom studied at MIT,

Harvard, Chicago, Cambridge, Oxford, and so on, where they all learned the same neoclassical theology. Part VI, 'On money', has some further comments on the World Bank.

The review of Martin Lewis's *Green Delusions* is included just to say something in response to the irritations of 'radical environmental chic' and the bad practice of criticizing people (me, for one, Paul Ehrlich for another), without first taking the trouble to read what they said.

3 Ultimate confusion: the economics of Julian Simon*

... scribbling nonsense and dispensing hollow verbiage that fundamentally and forever rots people's brains

Schopenhauer, referring to Hegel

Julian Simon frequently exaggerates and makes mistakes, and he has frequently been caught at it (see references). Yet he persists. Why? No doubt because he thinks he is right. However, by making mistakes faster than his critics can correct them, he also maintains a permanent debating advantage, at least in the media. In spite of the frustration of falling further behind in the thankless clean-up job, critics have no choice but to keep on exposing his errors and exaggerations. We cannot just ignore him because the Reagan administration takes him very seriously, as evidenced by his influence on the position taken by the USA at the United Nations Conference on Population held in Mexico City.

Simon's belief in unlimited growth, along with his antipathy to government (except when it subsidizes nuclear power), is exactly what Reagan and his many supporters want to hear – 'keep the government off the people's backs while they accumulate wealth'. Perhaps that was a reasonable view for a country engaged in settling an empty continent (forget the Indians). It is not a reasonable view for a crowded continent in which one man's production is another man's pollution, and someone else's depletion. So, in the spirit of perseverance in a worthy cause I list below a number of mistakes and exaggeratons, which, once reflected on by thoughtful people, should diminish the baleful influence of Mr Simon's popular ideas.

Simon's denial of resource finitude
This is the linchpin of Simon's position. In support of his view that 'resources are not meaningfully finite' he offers two arguments, one theoretical (largely semantic), and the other empirical.

The theoretical argument is that just as there are infinitely many points on a one-inch line segment, so too there are infinitely many lines of division separating copper from non-copper in the earth. Therefore copper is not countable. Therefore copper is infinite. Simon reasons

* Published in *Futures*, **17** (5), October 1985, pp. 446–50.

from infinite divisibility to infinite amount. But the infinite divisibility of a line segment does not imply infinite length. Infinitely many possible boundaries separating copper from non-copper do not imply an infinite amount of copper. It is a replay of Zeno's paradox of Achilles never catching up with the tortoise who had a finite head start. Simon would clearly have bet on the tortoise. Understandably some readers will think it unlikely that anyone would make that mistake, and will therefore suspect me of setting up a straw man. I beg such readers to turn to pages 47–9 of *The Ultimate Resource* and read them carefully.

The empirical argument is drawn largely from a study by Weinberg and Goeller, *The Age of Substitutability*, which Simon cites in support of his infinite substitutability premise. Even if copper were finite it could be thought of as if it were infinite because there are infinite possibilities of substituting other resources for copper. Of course if the set of all resources is finite, then infinite substitutability among resources does not render the set infinite. But more important than this logical glitch is what Simon omits to tell us, namely that Weinberg and Goeller's *Age of Substitutability* is a steady state. It assumes a constant population at 2.5 times the existing population with constant world energy use at 12 times present levels, implying a per capita world energy use of only 70 per cent of current US per capita use. The scenario assumes a low-cost, abundant energy source. Moreover, this high-consumption steady state is the maximum that Weinberg and Goeller consider technically feasible, and they caution that it would require planning on an unprecedented scale.

In other words, the very study that Simon appeals to for empirical support of his unlimited growth via the free market position specifically rejects the notion of unlimited growth, and further cautions that such a maximum consumption steady state could not be a creature of *laissez-faire*, but would require extensive planning. Such selective omissions of contrary evidence from the testimony of his own expert witnesses do not inspire confidence in Mr Simon's eagerness to tell the whole truth.

In sum, both the theoretical and empirical arguments against finitude fail utterly. Since everything else in Simon's position depends on abolishing finitude, the game is effectively over. But other issues less central to his position beg for attention.

Entropy doesn't exist
If environmental sources of raw material and sinks for waste were infinite, then it would not matter that the flow between them was entropic. Nor, if there were no such thing as entropy, would it matter if sources and sinks were finite, because recycling could be 100 per cent.

Once Simon has abolished finitude he logically does not need to deny the Second Law of Thermodynamics. But he does so anyway, for good measure:

> Let us work mainly with energy, the hardest case from my standpoint because it (almost alone among generic resources) cannot be totally recycled. (Simon, 1983, p. 57)

The clear implication is that most non-energy resources can be totally recycled, while energy can be recycled but not totally. This is wrong. No resource can be totally recycled, and energy cannot be recycled at all (except by expending more energy than the amount recycled). Simon considers the entropy constraint irrelevant because he does not understand it. He identifies entropy only with the ultimate heat death of the universe, not with the qualitative difference between equal quantities of raw material and waste. Entropy is a measure of that irreversible qualitative difference and is relevant to economics on a day-to-day basis, regardless of the ultimate heat death which we agree with Simon in not worrying about.

Ecology doesn't exist
Not a single chapter in *The Resourceful Earth* was written by an ecologist. Simon sees the natural world mainly as a source of vexations, not services. In an interview with Simon by William F. Buckley, Jr, we find the following exchange:

Simon:	... as you get greater population density, you get better transportation systems ...
Buckley:	You wipe out disease enclaves too, don't you?
Simon:	Pardon?
Buckley:	You wipe out disease enclaves – malarial forests and that kind of stuff.
Simon:	Absolutely. Thank you for mentioning it ...

It would seem that the only consequence of habitat destruction is to rid the world of malaria. (Actually cutting forests, at least initially, increases the incidence of malaria since it forces mosquitoes out of the high canopy down to the ground where man is.) But the very idea that we may lose a valuable natural service is absent. In a similar vein, Simon observes that environmentalists speak of 'wetlands lost', which he considers an example of persuasive labelling, whereas previously the same phenomenon was referred to, more objectively in Simon's view, as 'swamps drained' (Simon, 1981, p. 312).

Further evidence of the absence of biological understanding is provided by a stunning *non sequitur*. After citing the reasonable estimate
that one billion species have probably become extinct over the past 3.5
billion years, he says, 'If genetic extinction doomed mankind, presumably it would have died a billion deaths by now!' Again, some reader
probably suspects me of quoting out of context. Please read page 180
of *The Resourceful Earth*, and maybe you can make sense of it.

Population limits don't exist

Again, from the interview with Buckley (Buckley, 1982, p. 208):

> *Buckley*: All right. Now, probably the most controversial part of your thesis
> has to do of course with population. You find yourself asserting in effect
> that in as much as that which an individual creates is almost always more
> than that which he consumes, the greater the number of people who inhabit
> the globe, the greater the per capita production. Did I get it right?
> *Simon*: Yes.

The question is, did Simon get it right? Not by a long shot. To begin
with, even if everyone produces more than he consumes, it simply does
not follow that more people will raise per capita production. But that
is straining out gnats. The camel we are expected to swallow is the old
infinite-resources claim which of course settles the issue. How could
there be limits to population size, or anything else, if resources are
infinite? Since Simon's arguments against finitude of resources have
already been shown to be fallacious we need not waste time proving
that unlimited population growth is a bad policy. What is worth our
time is to inquire why Simon believes unlimited population growth is
desirable, as well as possible.

Misanthropy, double maximization and genius

Simon values human life, and thinks of neo-Malthusians as misanthrop-
ists. But most neo-Malthusians would agree with Simon that ten billion
people are better than two billion – as long as they are not all alive at
the same time! Neo-Malthusians want to maximize the cumulative total
of lives ever to be lived over time at a sufficient per capita standard for
a good life. Simon wants to maximize the number of people simultaneously alive. But too many people alive at once overshoots and
lowers carrying capacity, leading to fewer people in subsequent time
periods and a lower cumulative total over time. Of course, for Simon
these issues do not arise because he has simply declared carrying
capacity to be infinite.

Not content to maximize population, Simon further advocates

Bentham's 'greatest good for the greatest number', seemingly unaware of the mathematical impossibility of double maximization. Is there no trade-off between per capita consumption and number of people? If there is you can't maximize for both. But if resources are infinite then at least both can grow faster.

Nor for Simon is there any trade-off between present and future generations:

> Because we can expect future generations to be richer than we are, no matter what we do about resources, asking us to refrain from using resources now so that future generations can have them is like asking the poor to make gifts to the rich. (Simon, 1981, p. 15)

And while the poor should not be expected to make gifts to the rich, neither, it would seem, in a world of infinite resources, is there any reason for the rich to make gifts to the poor. Note the axiomatic nature of the belief that future generations must necessarily be richer. That, of course, presupposes the answer to the whole growth debate.

A further reason adduced by Simon for population growth is the 'genius argument'. With 4000 births there is a better chance of getting an Einstein or a Mozart than with only 40 births. Inept as this argument is in ignoring the unique combination of nature and nurture underlying genius, it should at least have occurred to Simon that the chances of getting another Hitler or Caligula likewise increase.

Some exaggerations
First:

> It is not entirely farfetched to compare this operation [use of US public funds for population control at home and abroad] to the CIA attempts to assassinate leaders and other persons in countries with which the US is at peace, without explicit approval of the American voters and taxpayers. (Simon, 1981, p. 297)

How about 'mostly' farfetched?

Second:

> The availability of energy has been increasing, and meaningful cost has been decreasing, over the entire span of humankind's history. We expect this benign trend to continue at least until our sun ceases to shine in perhaps 7 billion years, and until the exhaustion of the supply of elemental inputs for fission (and perhaps for fusion). (Simon, 1984, p. 25)

This is from one who accuses *Global 2000* of making sweeping extrapolations!

Third:

> You see, in the end, copper and oil come out of our minds. That's really where they are. (Buckley, 1982, p. 207)

One does not belittle the enormous capacities of the human mind by insisting that copper and oil are simply not ideas and really do come out of the ground. Indeed, to the extent that the human mind comes to conceive of itself as generating copper and oil out of itself, then we may legitimately claim that the mind has been depleted and polluted by 'hollow verbiage that fundamentally and forever rots people's brains'.

Optimal allocation vs optimal scale

The Resourceful Earth is Simon's attack on *Global 2000*. The fundamental difference between the two concerns the importance of the physical scale of the economy relative to the overall ecosystem. The economy, guided by a competitive market, will theoretically attain a Pareto-optimum allocation of resources (a condition in which no one can be made better off without someone being made worse off). That is the best we can hope for from the market. But optimal allocation of resources within the economy is one thing, and optimal physical scale of the entire economy relative to the ecosystem is something else. Nothing in the market system guarantees the latter. The scale of population and per capita resource use can be doubled or halved and the market will still find an optimal allocation. The inherent growth bias of the market, especially as supplemented by Keynesian policies, will push us beyond optimal sustainable scale. But the market will keep on optimally allocating resources. The market will always be making the best of an increasingly bad situation. Relative scarcities (one resource relative to another) will always be properly measured by prices, but absolute scarcity (of all resources in general relative to the ecosystem) will increase without being registered in relative prices. For *Global 2000* this was the issue. As we grow beyond optimal scale, absolute scarcity increases, but the price system cannot, by itself, reflect the absolute dimension of scarcity.

For Simon, of course, absolute scarcity doesn't exist since resources are infinite. For Simon the economic optimum coincides with a physical maximum. This by itself is very surprising and should make us sceptical.

When we are also told that the physical maximum can approach infinity, our scepticism should harden into rejection.

References

Buckley, William, (1982), Interview with Julian Simon, *Population and Development Review*, **8** (1), March, pp. 205–18.

Daly, Herman E., (1982), 'Review of *The Ultimate Resource*', *Bulletin of the Atomic Scientists*, January, pp. 39–42.

Daly, Herman E., (1984), 'Review of *The Resourceful Earth*', *Environment*, **26** (7), September, pp. 25–8.

Ehrlich, Paul and Anne, (1985), 'Review of *The Resourceful Earth*', *Bulletin of the Atomic Scientists*, February, pp. 44–7.

Population and Development Review (1982), 'Review symposium on *The Ultimate Resource*', March, pp. 163–77.

Simon, Julian, (1981), *The Ultimate Resource*, Princeton, NJ: Princeton University Press.

Simon, Julian and Kahn, Herman (eds) (1984), *The Resourceful Earth*, Oxford: Basil Blackwell.

Simon, Julian, (1983), 'In defense: The ultimate resource', *Bulletin of the Atomic Scientists*, May, pp. 57–9.

4 Free market environmentalism: turning a good servant into a bad master*

Free Market Environmentalism, by Terry L. Anderson and Donald R. Leal (San Francisco: Pacific Research Institute, 1991), reaffirms the virtue of full-cost pricing – that is, the doctrine that prices should reflect full marginal social opportunity costs. The focus is specifically on environmental costs rather than social costs in general, but the principle of internalizing external costs has been applied in many areas. The environment especially suffers when government intervenes to subsidize consumption, whether of water by farmers in the western USA, or of cleared land by cattle ranchers in the Brazilian Amazon.

Hayek, yes – but what about Coase and Pigou?

Allocation by decentralized market decision making is much better than centrally planned allocation, for reasons well expressed long ago by F.A. Hayek, and that cannot be restated too often. Although this principle has been well known for a long time, it is amazing how routinely we violate it in practice, and the authors deserve credit for pointing this out with specific examples, largely drawn from the American West. The book has many important lessons for those who think that the market is always the enemy of the environment.

The problem of internalizing social and environmental costs has a long history of discussion in economics. There are two main alternative approaches to internalizing external costs, the Pigouvian and the Coasean, after their two champions, A.C. Pigou[1] and R.H. Coase.[2] Pigou advocated the imposition of taxes or subsidies to close the gap between social cost (or benefit) and private cost (or benefit). Coase advocated the definition or redefinition of property rights in such a way that bargaining among private citizens would lead to the incorporation of formerly external costs in decisions. He demonstrated that from the point of view of efficiency the important thing is that someone should own the rights to use, say, air and water. Whether ownership was vested in those wanting to use the environment as a source of clean inputs, or as a sink for waste outputs, was not important as a matter of efficiency,

* Published in *Critical Review*, **6** (2–3), 1993, pp. 171–83. The ideas and opinions expressed in this review are those of the reviewer and should in no way be attributed to the World Bank.

although it certainly was an equity issue. Anderson and Leal clearly favour the Coasean over the Pigouvian approach. I do not at all criticize them for that, but I do think it is wrong to equate the Pigouvian approach with central planning, and the Coasean approach with the free market. This is in effect what they do (Anderson and Leal, 1991, p. 67), but I cannot give definitive citations since they make not even the most passing of references to either Coase or Pigou. The lack of historical grounding of their work is distressing.

What is unfortunate is that they mistake this important part of the truth for the whole truth – the *pars pro toto* fallacy, to indict them in Latin for their crime against reason. Their vision of the economic problem is also partial – they see it entirely as the problem of self-interested individuals acting on the basis of diffuse knowledge (ibid., p. 5). Hayek has shown that this is indeed an important part of the problem – how to use diffuse, ephemeral knowledge not given in its totality to anyone. The market can use such knowledge; central planners cannot. And surely we are all self-interested.

But there is much more to it. This self that interests us so much is in reality not an isolated atom, but is constituted by its relations in community with others – the very identity of the self is social rather than atomistic. If the very self is constituted by relations of community, then self-interest can no longer be atomistically self-contained or defined independently of the community. While some knowledge is diffuse and ephemeral, and it is a great virtue of the market that it can tap that knowledge, other knowledge is quite public, universal, and fairly permanent – the laws of thermodynamics, for example, or the knowledge that murder and theft are wrong. To insist that everything is reducible to atomistic, selfish individuals acting to maximize their gain on the basis of diffuse, piecemeal knowledge locked in their separate sealed heads is to treat an abstraction as more real than the concrete experience from which it has been abstracted. More about that later.

The cattleman's paradigm: fencing and branding
The book argues that when private costs diverge too much from social (environmental) costs, property rights and technology usually evolve to bring them back into conformity. There is very little if any need for government to intervene to internalize external costs – economic and technological evolution will do it for us. All environmental problems can be solved by some high-tech analogue to the fencing of land or the branding of cattle. These new property-defining technologies will evolve in the future, just as fencing and branding evolved in the past in the Far West, to give property-rights solutions to environmental problems.

Wolves can be 'fenced' with a radio-activated collar (p. 34) that injects the animal with a tranquillizer when it crosses an electronic barrier so that it may be returned to its designated habitat (presumably the habitat owned or rented by its owner). Whales can be 'branded' by genetic prints and monitored by satellites that would establish a mechanism for enforcing property rights in whales (p. 34). If you want to save the whales you can go buy some – and then spend all of your time and money in court enforcing your property right against whoever damages your whales with pollutants that have also been chemically 'branded' and rendered traceable. Perhaps you could even sue another whale owner over custody of offspring. Litigation to establish the property rights of whale owners relative to krill owners will certainly enrich the lawyers.

Since the focus is on property rights it is important to ask where these rights come from and how they are established. Here we get two conflicting stories. The dominant story is that property rights evolve as a result of entrepreneurial initiative.

'It is important to recognize that any case of external benefits or costs provides fertile ground for an entrepreneur who can define and enforce property rights' (p. 21). Again we are reminded that 'even externalities offer profit niches to the environmental entrepreneur who can define and enforce property rights to the unowned resource and charge the free-riding user' (p. 23). Clearly, it is the entrepreneur who, in the authors' view, both defines and enforces property rights. Further clarification is provided by a historical example of how this was done in the Far West:

> I, the undersigned, do hereby notify the public that I claim the valley, branching off the Glendive Creek, four miles east of the Allard, and extending to its source on the south side of the Northern Pacific Railroad as a stock range. – Chas. S. Johnson (no date given)

Thus did Mr Johnson define his property rights. Exactly how he intended to enforce those claims against other strong-willed individuals he left to the reader's imagination. Anderson and Leal also leave to our imagination just how this example might be replicated today. My imagination suggests the following:

> I, the undersigned, do hereby notify the public that I claim all the air and space above my house. Trespassing airplanes and birds whose owners have not paid for the right of transit will be shot down by one of two Exocet missiles that are also my property.

Have I hereby become an environmental entrepreneur?

Is there no role at all for government in defining and enforcing property rights? Not in Chapters 2 and 3. However, in Chapter 11 a more reasonable line is offered. We are told that:

> As a definer and enforcer of property rights, government has an important role to play in this free market solution. Just as states registered cattle brands and prosecuted rustlers, the government could move us in the direction of free market environmentalism if it would register pollutants, monitor the flow of pollutants in the atmosphere, and enforce liability for damage. (p. 166)

Some rather important functions of the entrepreneur in Chapters 2 and 3 have, in Chapter 11, quite reasonably, but without explanation, been transferred to the government.

We are told that fencing the atmosphere 'to solve global commons problems' seems as unfathomable today 'as fencing the range seemed in 1840' (p. 165). What barbed wire did for enclosing the range 'lasimetrics' (p. 166, presumably referring to a laser-based surveying technology) will do for enclosing the atmosphere. I doubt it. People in 1840 knew all about fences. Barbed wire was a cheap fencing material, not a conceptual breakthrough. Even with lasimetrics, apportioning the atmosphere into private property remains unfathomable to anyone who tries to think it through.

The authors' 'quite simple' (p. 165) example for making clear the benefits of free market environmentalism in solving the problem of greenhouse gas emissions is privatization of highway ownership. Strict liability enforced on the highway owner would give the owner an incentive to control emissions (charge users accordingly), or to refuse access to high-polluting cars. No mention is made of the army of private guards and emissions inspectors required, nor the time lost in inspection and litigation. More important, one might have expected 'free market' economists to be a bit more sensitive to the problems of monopoly ownership – or are we to envision many parallel highways competing for the motorist? And if they compete, might they not compete by fudging emissions standards? We are back to government inspectors. Indeed we never got away from government since the emission standards have to be defined and enforced, and presumably this requires government – although, as we have seen, Chapters 2 and 3 leave these functions to the entrepreneur. Would not a stiff (Pigouvian) energy tax levied at the mine mouth or wellhead be a lot simpler?

Generalizing the 'bubble' concept

Not all policies offered are as weird as those discussed above, which the authors offer as solutions to the 'tougher problems' (p. 154). It is not clear that they consider the tougher problems to be real since they voice the suspicion that global warming may be 'hot air' (p. 159) or, worse, a fear 'used to drive sustainable development policies where nearly all resource use would be controlled by government' (p. 161). However, for more tractable problems, the paradigm policy of their free market environmentalism – the bubble concept, which limits aggregate polluting emissions in a region and then allows market exchange to allocate the quota among alternative users – is one that I wholeheartedly support. With obvious caveats about political acceptability, I would even suggest applying the same scheme to population control by setting up tradable reproduction rights corresponding in aggregate amount to replacement fertility, as proposed originally by Kenneth Boulding.[3] Anderson and Leal apparently see no connection between population growth and environmental problems so they do not discuss this application of the basic institution they advocate.

I make a point of mentioning Boulding's unpopular suggestion for two reasons. First, I believe that it was the earliest exposition of the economic logic underlying the bubble concept – that is, conformity to an aggregate limit with the minimum sacrifice of freedom and variability at the individual level. Boulding applied it to the area where it was politically least likely to be accepted. Second, the omission of population from a book on the environment has to be noted. All we are given by way of explanation is a reference to Julian Simon and the statement that 'the human mind . . . has allowed us to avoid Malthusian cycles' (p. 2). Some of 'us', some of the time, have indeed avoided the Malthusian trap, but currently half the world is caught in it. As will be discussed later, free trade makes it impossible to avoid spillovers from those caught in the Malthusian trap.

The authors recognize, but do not emphasize, that the bubble concept and its variants absolutely require an initial social, collective decision limiting the aggregate use of an environmental source or sink to an amount judged to be within environmental carrying capacity. They feel that it would be much better if the scale could be set by some kind of individualistic (Coasean) bargaining process rather than by collective decision. Their hope or faith is that the requisite property rights will somehow evolve in a way that makes this feasible (p. 147). In the meantime they reluctantly accept the political decision limiting scale as a necessary evil. A discussion of the roles of private versus public property in a broad Coasean framework would have been interesting, as would a discussion of the relative advantages of the Coasean and Pigouvian strategies of internalization. But, as lamented earlier, neither Coase nor Pigou even figures among the references.

Once scale has been set, another political decision must be made about the initial distribution of this newly created right among users. It may belong to the government initially, and then be allocated by auction to private users, who are in turn free to reallocate by sale or gift. Or the initial distribution may be to private parties, but this requires a political decision regarding to whom it should be given. Only after the community or the state establishes the right, and provides an initial distribution of its ownership, do we arrive at the 'free' market and its ability to reallocate the initial distribution. I think it would be more descriptive to call this '*constrained* market environmentalism' (ecologically and ethically constrained), but the authors want to call it '*free* market environmentalism'. The important thing, in my view, is to separate cleanly the collective decision on optimal (sustainable) scale of use of resources from the individualistic market decisions governing the optimal allocation of that total amount of resources among alternative uses. By scale I mean total resource use (population times per capita resource use); by sustainable scale I mean one that is within environmental carrying capacity.

Allocation, distribution and scale
The great virtue of the tradable permits scheme is that it forces us to distinguish three independent policy goals and to recognize that they require three independent policy instruments.[4] The goals are: (1) *allocation* – the division of the resource flow among alternative product uses; (2) *distribution* – the division of the resource flow, embodied in products, among different people; (3) *scale* – the total volume of the resource flow, the matter–energy throughput taken from the environment as low-entropy resources and returned to the environment as high-entropy wastes. Scale is relative to environmental carrying capacity.

Economic theory tells us that relative prices formed by supply and demand in competitive markets lead to an efficient allocation. Economic theory also tells us that there is a different efficient allocation for every initial distribution of ownership, so that justice or fairness of distribution is a separate goal from efficiency and requires a separate policy instrument – transfer payments such as welfare, social insurance, inheritance taxes, and so on. As for scale, it is largely ignored by standard economic theory, which has implicitly assumed that environmental sources and sinks were infinite. Consequently there is in economic theory no policy instrument for keeping scale within carrying capacity – nothing analogous to the Plimsoll line or load limit mark on a ship. If theorists recognize sustainable scale as a goal, then they are in the position of trying to kill three birds with two stones.

But the third stone, the scale limit, the economic Plimsoll line,[5] is evolving in practice ahead of theory. The beauty of the tradable permits scheme is that *first* we must face the scale question and draw a Plimsoll line at the amount of aggregate pollution (or depletion) that is ecologically sustainable. Second, rights to pollute (or deplete) up to that limited amount must be distributed in some fair manner. Only after these two political steps can market trading attain the efficient allocation. The market is 'free' only after its ecological and distributional boundaries have been politically established.

The distribution and scale questions are just as much *economic* as the allocation question in that they all involve the comparison of costs and benefits. But the dimensions on which costs and benefits are defined are different in each of the three cases. Allocative prices do not measure the costs and benefits of scale expansion, nor do they measure the costs and benefits of a more equal distribution of income or wealth. We have three different optima requiring three different policy instruments. In each case an optimum is formally defined by the equality of falling benefits and rising costs at the margin. But the definitions and measures of costs and benefits in each of the three cases are different because the problems to whose solution they are instrumental are different. The relative prices of shoes and bicycles are instrumental in allocating resources efficiently between shoes and bicycles, but are clearly not instrumental for deciding the proper range of inequality in wealth and income, nor for deciding how many people consuming how much per capita of natural resources gives the optimal scale.

Distribution and scale involve relationships with the poor, the future, and other species – relationships that are more social than individual in nature. *Homo economicus*, whether the self-contained atom of methodological individualism or the pure social automaton of collectivist ideology, is in either case a severe abstraction. Our concrete experience is that of 'persons in community'. We are individual persons, but our very individual identity is defined by the quality of our social relations. Our relations to each other are not just external, they are also internal – that is, the nature of the related entities (ourselves in this case) changes when relations among them change. We are related not only by the external nexus of individual willingnesses to pay for different things, but also by relations of kinship, friendship, citizenship, and trusteeship for the poor, the future, and other species. The attempt to abstract from all these relationships a *Homo economicus* whose identity is constituted only by individualistic willingness to pay is a distortion of our concrete experience as persons in community – an example of what A.N. Whitehead called the 'fallacy of misplaced concreteness'.[6]

The prices that measure the opportunity costs of reallocation are unrelated to measures of the opportunity costs of redistribution, or of a change in scale. Any trade-off among the three goals (for example, an improvement of distribution in exchange for a worsening in scale or allocation, or a more efficient allocation resulting from the harsher incentives of a less equal distribution of income) involves an ethical judgement about the quality of our social relations, rather than a calculation of our willingness to pay. The contrary view – that this choice among the three separate policy goals, and consequently the social relations that help to define us as persons – should be made on the basis of individual willingness to pay, just as the allocative trade-off between chewing gum and shoelaces is made, seems to be dominant in economics today. It is part of the retrograde modern reduction of all ethical choice to the level of personal tastes weighted by income.

It is much easier to correct the misunderstanding of the 'green critics' of tradable permits, who condemn them as 'licences to pollute'. They fail to recognize that the main point is to limit aggregate pollution to a sustainable level, and that the market is only allowed to allocate that fixed level, in an efficient manner, subject to a socially decided initial distribution. One reason the greens have not understood this is that economists have downplayed the scale and distribution parts of the tradable permit plans, focusing almost exclusively on their allocative superiority to command-and-control regulatory standards.

Alternative cattleman's paradigm: carrying capacity and sustainable development

'Carrying capacity', like branding and fencing, is also a cattleman's term relevant to the Far West, but unlike 'branding' it does not appear in the book's index, and certainly does not haunt the authors' imaginations in the way that branding and fencing do. In fact the book's concluding section on sustainable development leads one to conclude that the authors reject the concept of carrying capacity, or at least that they refuse to generalize it in the way they do branding and fencing. How they can advocate tradable permits as the main policy of 'free market environmentalism' without discussing carrying capacity is an inconsistency they never attempt to resolve.

The authors claim that sustainable development, in its 'more extreme versions' (p. 168), means that non-renewable resources should never be extracted. This is simply fatuous. No reference is provided to anyone holding such a position. The principle actually put forward by many advocates of sustainable development is that non-renewable resources be depleted at a rate equal to the rate at which renewable substitutes are developed. Differences emerge about how broadly or narrowly to define substitute (for example, most would consider an increase in copper recycling as a substitute for the discovery of more copper). Quite sophisticated accounting principles for separating the rents from non-renewable resource extraction into a capital component (to be reinvested in renewable substitutes) and an income component (available for current consumption) have been developed.[7]

Even if there were a non-renewable resource for which there are no substitutes, no one advocates leaving it for ever in the ground, although many certainly do advocate sharing it over some number of generations greater than one. Anderson and Leal see no need for such sharing since they advocate Barnett and Morse's[8] intergenerational invisible hand, the doctrine which holds that 'by devoting itself to improving the lot of the living . . . each generation . . . transmits a more productive world to those who follow'. How fortunate! We can forget about intergenerational sharing and maximize for the present, just as we can forget about intragenerational sharing and maximize for ourselves. In both cases we are comforted by the augmented invisible hand that transforms private (and present) greed into public (and future) benevolence. We have here, in T.S. Eliot's mordant words, 'a system so perfect that no one needs to be good'.

In contrast to the 'intergenerational invisible hand' consider the statement by Nicholas Georgescu-Roegen that,

> Every time we produce a Cadillac we irrevocably destroy an amount of low entropy that could otherwise be used for producing a plow or a spade. In other words, every time we produce a Cadillac we do it at the cost of decreasing the number of human lives in the future.[9]

Just why free market environmentalists believe that Barnett and Morse are right and Georgescu-Roegen is wrong would have made for an interesting discussion. But Georgescu-Roegen joins Coase and Pigou in the distinguished company of authors of unnoticed classics which Anderson and Leal might have used to deepen and enrich their analysis.

The authors see no possible conflict between economic growth and the environment: 'Higher incomes allow us to afford more environmental quality in addition to material goods' (p. 171). Everyone will readily agree that if we are richer, then all our problems, including environmental ones, will be easier to solve. That is hardly in dispute.

What is at issue is whether economic growth at the present margin, as currently measured, is really making us richer. If the marginal production benefits of growth are less than the marginal environmental costs made necessary by the production increase, then growth as currently measured is making us poorer, not richer. The authors seem blind to the very possibility of growth that costs more than it is worth at the margin, just as they seem blind to any possible intergenerational conflict of interest.

Free market and free trade?

What does 'free market environmentalism' have to say about free trade and the environment? Nothing, although free trade is certainly an important part of the overall free market position, allowing the export of production in exchange for the import of carrying capacity from other countries. This is a critical omission. Suppose a country follows the path of internalizing external costs (environmental and social) into prices that consequently tell the truth, in so far as possible, about real sacrifices. Whether this is done by Pigouvian or Coasean strategies does not matter. Now imagine free trade (including free capital mobility) with a country that allows firms to externalize such costs. The firms in the first country with truthful, higher prices will be undercut by firms in the second country with deceptive, lower prices. Should not the first country be allowed a countervailing tariff to protect, *not an inefficient industry, but an efficient national policy of full-cost pricing*? So far the free traders, including GATT, and the free market environmentalists, have not been able to resolve this issue. Anderson and Leal simply ignore it.

This defect may stem in part from not recognizing the population problem. Free trade between high-wage and low-wage countries will tend to equalize wages, and if capital is mobile internationally this tendency will be very strong. Low-wage countries tend to be already overpopulated and to have high rates of population growth, especially among the labouring class. With free trade and capital mobility the wage-reducing consequences of high population growth in low-wage countries will spill over into high-wage countries. The effect on wages and profits in high-wage countries will be the same as under free migration of labour – wages will fall as profits rise. If a country wants to follow a high-wage policy at home and avoid extreme inequality in incomes, it cannot, in effect, erase its borders with low-wage countries.[10] It is unavailing to appeal to the doctrine of 'comparative advantage' and its comforting conclusions because that doctrine is explicitly premised on the immobility of capital internationally.[11]

International competition to lower costs can be 'efficiency-increasing', but it can also be 'standards-lowering'. The standards that get lowered in free trade with free capital mobility are mainly the standards of living of workers, but also include environmental standards, health insurance, safety standards, and so on. Anderson and Leal are not alone in ignoring these issues that have been studiously avoided by mainstream economists.

Anderson and Leal use the partial truth that full-cost pricing is a good thing in order to bludgeon other partial truths that are not really contradictory to the piece of the truth that they have managed to grasp. Where full-cost pricing is in contradiction to other parts of the free market ideology, as with free trade, they ignore the issue. In this case, the market needs protection from its ideological friends more than from its leftist enemies. The latter are now justly discredited. The clear and present danger to the market comes from the exaggerated enthusiasm for a world in which everything is either fenced or branded and bought and sold for private profit by environmental entrepreneurs bent on defining and enforcing 'their' property rights. With no collective decisions or community consensus about ecological limits to economic expansion and ethical limits to the concentration of ownership of eco-logical space, we will spend all our energies in litigation to 'evolve' and defend our individual property rights against the conflicts generated by continued economic expansion within a finite ecosystem. The market as an institution for allocating scarce resources will be deprived of the sustainable ecological context in which its virtue, efficiency, can shine. An efficient servant will become an unjust and unsustainable master.

Notes

1. A.C. Pigou, *The Economics of Welfare*, London: Macmillan, 1920.
2. R.H. Coase, 'The Problem of Social Cost', *Journal of Law and Economics*, **3** (1988): 1–44.
3. Kenneth E. Boulding, *The Meaning of the Twentieth Century*, New York: Harper and Row, 1963.
4. Jan Tinbergen, *On the Theory of Economic Policy*, Amsterdam: North Holland Press, 1952.
5. Herman E. Daly, 'Elements of Environmental Macroeconomics', in Robert Costanza (ed.), *Ecological Economics*, New York: Columbia University Press, 1991.
6. Herman E. Daly and John B. Cobb, Jr, *For the Common Good*, Boston: Beacon Press, 1989.
7. Salah El Serafy, 'Substainability, Income Measurement, and Growth', in Robert Goodland et al. (eds), *Population, Technology, and Lifestyle*, Washington, DC: Island Press, 1992.
8. Harold Barnett and Chandler Morse, *Scarcity and Growth*, Baltimore: Johns Hopkins University Press, 1963.
9. Nicholas Georgescu-Roegen, 'The Entropy Law and the Economic Problem', in

Herman E. Daly (ed.), *Economics, Ecology, Ethics*, San Francisco: W.H. Freeman and Co., 1980.
10. William Greider, *Who Will Tell the People?*, New York: Simon and Schuster, 1992, ch. 7.
11. See reference in note 6 above, especially ch. II.

5 Review of Wilfred Beckerman's *Small is Stupid: Blowing the Whistle on the Greens* (Duckworth, 1995)*

The premise of this small book is not nearly as stupid as that of Wilfred Beckerman's earlier book, *In Defence of Economic Growth* (1974).[1] One can find in it many sensible statements, such as: '[N]o doubt tougher policies to protect the environment in all forms should be implemented' (p. 38). Beckerman even has a few nice words for E.J. Mishan and his pioneering book *The Costs of Economic Growth*, as well as for E.F. Schumacher, in spite of the derogatory use made of the title of the latter's book *Small is Beautiful*. After all, Mishan is an economist, and so was Schumacher, so they can be held up as evidence of how reasonable economists are in order to further confuse the 'deep ecologists', who, let it be admitted, sometimes seem as deeply confused as Beckerman pictures them. But, let us not forget that the mainstream economists heatedly rejected these works of Mishan and Schumacher, and so does Beckerman, after first making his rather ingratiating use of them (p. 3).

The words 'population' and 'demography' do not appear in the index, which is partly due to the lack of attention paid to these subjects in the book and partly due to sloppy indexing, because there is in fact some discussion of population. This consists mainly of an uncritical reaffirmation of the demographic transition hypothesis in its crudest form, namely that economic growth will automatically limit population growth (p. 63). This is important to note, because the book is really a generalization of the demographic transitionist policy-by-correlation theme. Whatever the problem, its solution is correlated with economic growth, and therefore its solution *is* economic growth. For example, we are told, 'If you want to increase the proportion of the population with access to clean drinking water, get richer' (p. 41). No one denies that problems are easier to solve if you are rich than if you are poor. So the issue is, how to become rich?

By economic growth, of course, is Beckerman's answer. But does economic growth, as currently measured, and starting from the present margin, really make us richer? Might it not conceivably make us poorer by increasing uncounted environmental costs faster than it increases

* Published in *Population and Development Review*, **21** (3), September 1995, pp. 665–73.

counted production benefits? If economic growth were defined as growth for which inclusive marginal benefits are greater than inclusive marginal costs, then it would be a tautology to say that economic growth makes us richer. However, we would then have to recognize the concept of anti-economic growth – growth for which inclusive marginal costs are greater than inclusive marginal benefits, growth that makes us poorer and therefore makes all problems harder to solve. Clearly anti-economic growth is conceivable, and Beckerman correctly points out that the economist A.C. Pigou raised the issue many years ago.[2]

Because non-monetary (ecological and social) costs are unmeasurable, Beckerman follows other economists in ignoring them, once their theoretical existence is acknowledged. The assumption is that non-monetary costs and benefits are small compared with monetary costs and benefits, and will remain so. Much of Beckerman's discussion is devoted to trying to provide evidence for the plausibility of this assumption and for prevailing low estimates of monetary costs of environmental disruption. One of his least convincing arguments in this regard is that since agriculture accounts for only 3 per cent of gross national product in the USA, and greenhouse-gas induced climate change affects only agriculture, there is little to worry about. To clarify the point, he tells us that 'even if the net output of agriculture fell by 50 per cent by the end of the next century this is only a 1.5 per cent cut in GNP' (p. 91). Imagine Beckerman's reaction if an environmentalist had assumed constant prices in the face of a 50 per cent reduction in agricultural output – a good whose demand is famously inelastic!

Beckerman does not distinguish growth (quantitative increase in resource throughput) from development (qualitative improvement in efficiency of resource use). Of course GNP also lumps these dissimilar categories together, so Beckerman is following tradition while perpetuating the likelihood of confusion. Ecologists are talking about limits to *growth*. Beckerman counters with a long list of true but irrelevant examples of how *development* has increased welfare, such as the invention of the polio vaccine or fibre optics.

The concept of anti-economic growth seems to economists an empty box – theoretically definable, but empirically irrelevant. But a moment's reflection shows that microeconomics is about nothing else than expanding each activity of production or consumption up to its optimum, and then stopping growth before it becomes anti-economic. All micro activities reach a point beyond which further growth raises costs more than benefits. Microeconomics seeks to discover the optimum scale of an activity, the point at which its growth should stop. But when we move to macroeconomics (growth in GNP), we find no concept of an optimum scale for the macroeconomy. The macro-economy is thought to be the whole. Therefore it has no optimum scale beyond which it gets too big relative to something else, making further growth anti-economic. How is it possible that each micro activity has an optimal scale while the aggregate of those activities does not?

I think it is because at the micro level growth of one activity is limited by non-growth or slower growth of other complementary activities and by the disproportionalities that result. But if all activities grow proportionally, then economists see no limit. One way for an activity (for example, an industry) to grow proportionally is to add identical units (firms). And population grows by adding additional people who are close replicas of existing people. There is no fixed factor; everything can grow proportionally for ever. Of course, to one who sees the economy as a subsystem of an ecosystem that is finite, non-growing, and materially closed, something *is* fixed, and the vision of perpetual growth of the subsystem is absurd. Yes, there is a throughput of solar energy, but that too is finite and non-growing.

For Beckerman and most mainstreamers, however, the economy is not the subsystem, it is the total system; the 'environment' is the sub-system, a sector of the economy to which resources can be allocated just like any other sector (pp. 121–2). And resources are not finite in any meaningful sense (p. 49). Therefore if the environment provides a bottleneck, we invest more resources in the environment sector, thereby removing that disproportionality, just as with any other sector.

In my view everything depends on which paradigm one accepts: the economy as subsystem or the economy as total system. For those who, understandably, have come to object to the word 'paradigm', I suggest Joseph Schumpeter's earlier and more descriptive term, 'pre-analytic vision'. Since I think this pre-analytic vision is fundamental, I will take the time to illustrate it with a story about the evolution of the World Bank's 1992 *World Development Report*, subtitled *Development and the Environment*. Since Beckerman was the major external adviser to the Bank team that wrote the report, and since he draws on its contents heavily in parts of the book under review, the story is very much to the point.

An early draft of the 1992 *WDR* had a diagram entitled 'The relation-ship between the economy and the environment'. It consisted simply of a square labelled 'economy' – with an arrow entering labelled 'inputs' and an arrow exiting labelled 'outputs'. I worked in the Environment Department of the World Bank at that time, and was asked to review and comment on the draft. I suggested that the diagram was a good idea, but failed to show the environment, and that it would help to have a larger box, representing the environment, that contained the smaller box representing the economy. Then the relation between the environment and the economy would be clear – specifically that the economy is a subsystem of the environment and depends on it both as a source of raw material inputs and as a sink for waste outputs.

The second draft had the same diagram and text, but with an unlabelled box drawn around the economy, like a picture frame. I commented that the larger box had to be labelled 'environment' and that the text had to explain that the economy was related to the environment as a subsystem of the larger ecosystem. The next draft omitted the diagram altogether. There was no further effort to depict the relation of the economy to the environment. I thought that was very odd.

By coincidence a few months later the Chief Economist of the World Bank, Lawrence Summers, under whom the 1992 *WDR* was being written, was on a review panel at the Smithsonian Institution discussing the book *Beyond the Limits*,[3] which he considered worthless. That book contained a diagram showing the relation of the economy to the ecosystem as subsystem to total system, similar to what I had suggested. In the question-and-answer time I asked Summers whether, looking at that diagram, he felt the issue of the physical size of the economic subsystem relative to the total ecosystem was important, and whether economists should be asking, 'What is the optimal scale of the macroeconomy relative to the environment that supports it?' His reply was immediate and definite. 'That's not the right way to look at it,' he said.

Reflecting on these two experiences has strengthened my belief that the difference lies in our 'pre-analytic visions'. My pre-analytic vision of the economy as subsystem leads immediately to the questions: How big is the subsystem relative to the total system? How big can it be without disrupting the functioning of the total system? How big should it be: what is its optimal scale beyond which further growth would be anti-economic, would cost more than it is worth? The World Bank's Chief Economist had no intention of being engaged by these subversive questions – that is not the right way to look at it, and any questions arising from that way of looking at it are invalid.

It sounds unreasonable, but such had also been my response to the draft diagram showing the economy receiving raw material inputs from nowhere and exporting waste outputs to nowhere. That is not the right way to look at it, I said, and any questions arising from that picture – say, how to make the economy grow as fast as possible by speeding up throughput – were invalid. Unless one has the pre-analytic vision of the economy as subsystem, the very idea of sustainable development – of a subsystem being sustained by a larger system whose carrying capacity it must respect – makes no sense. The pre-analytic vision of the economy as a box floating in infinite space allows people to speak of 'sustainable growth' – a clear oxymoron to those who see the economy as a sub-system. The difference could not be more fundamental, or more irreconcilable.

It is interesting that so much should be at stake in a simple picture. Once you draw the boundary of the environment around the economy, you have implicitly admitted that the economy cannot expand for ever. You have said that John Stuart Mill was right, that populations of human bodies and populations of capital goods cannot grow indefinitely. At some point growth must give way to development as the path of progress, and we must come to terms with Mill's stationary state.

But the World Bank cannot say that – at least not yet and not publicly – because growth is the official solution to poverty. If growth is physically limited or begins to cost more than it is worth, then how will we lift poor people out of poverty? The answer is painfully obvious: by population control; by redistribution; and by technical improvements in resource productivity. But population control and redistribution are considered politically impossible. Increasing resource productivity is considered a good idea until we realize that we have bought high productivity and high incomes for capital and labour by using resources lavishly, thereby sacrificing resource productivity. Yet resources are the limiting factor in the long run – the very factor whose productivity economic logic says should be maximized. When we draw a containing boundary of the environment around the economy, we move from 'empty-world' economics to 'full-world' economics. Economic logic stays the same, but the perceived pattern of scarcity changes radically, and policies must change radically. That is why there is such resistance to a simple picture. The fact that the picture is so simple and so obviously realistic is why it cannot be contemplated by the growth economists – 'that's not the right way to look at it!'

Beckerman recognizes the issue of scale, but only to dismiss it. After acknowledging the distinction between optimal allocation and optimal scale, and the fact that the price system solves the allocation problem but not the scale problem, he states, correctly. 'This would not matter if there were no environmental limits to the total scale of world output' (p. 142). Are there in fact such limits? No, says Beckerman, claiming to have disposed of the problems of finitude, entropy and dependence on photosynthesis in Part I. Without environmental limits there can be no problem of scale. No error of logic here, just a colossal misperception of fact!

Beckerman's other attempt to deal with the scale question comes in an interesting comment on a statement co-authored by E.O. Wilson and Paul Ehrlich: 'The indispensable strategy for saving our fellow living creatures and ourselves in the long run is . . . to reduce the scale of human activity' (cited on p. 74). Beckerman then chides Wilson for having also argued that biodiversity provides crops, timber, pulp, petroleum substitutes, and so on – all grist to the mill of economic activity. Beckerman asks, 'What would be the point of reducing economic activity in order to provide a better basis for increasing it?' (ibid.). I do not know what Wilson's answer would be, but mine is that the object of preserving biodiversity is not to *increase* economic activity, but to be able to *continue* it into the future at some constant, sustainable level. This brings us to the question of sustainable development, a concept for which Beckerman has little use.

Beckerman's discussion of sustainable development in Chapter 9 provides some useful clarifications and a good occasion for making a few more. Since I advocate what he calls the 'sustainability as constraint' position, I begin with the dilemma in which he claims to have placed those like me:

> The advocates of sustainable development as a constraint, therefore, face a dilemma. Either they stick to 'strong' sustainability, which is logical, but requires them to subscribe to a morally repugnant and totally impracticable objective, or they switch to some welfare-based concept of sustainability, in which case they are advocating a concept that appears to be redundant and unable to qualify as a logical constraint on welfare maximisation. (p. 137)

I advocate strong sustainability, thereby receiving Beckerman's blessing in the realm of logic while provoking his indignation in the realms of morality and practicality. Consequently I will craft a reply to those charges. But first, I congratulate him for his effective demolition of 'weak sustainability'. I hope he has more success than I have had in converting the many environmental economists who still cling to it.

Beckerman's concept of strong sustainability, however, is one he has made up in order to serve as a straw man. In the literature weak sustainability assumes that man-made and natural capital are basically substitutes. He got that right. Strong sustainability assumes that man-made and natural capital are basically complements. Beckerman completely missed that one. He thinks strong sustainability means that no species should ever become extinct, nor any non-renewable resource ever be taken from the ground, no matter how many people are starving. I have referred to that concept as 'absurdly strong sustainability' in order to dismiss it, so as to focus on the relevant issue: namely, are man-made and natural capital substitutes or complements? That is really what is at issue between strong and weak sustainability. Since Beckerman got the definition right for weak sustainability, his arguments against it are relevant and, as I said above, convincing. But since he got the definition of strong sustainability wrong, in spite of the obvious symmetry of the cases, his arguments against it are irrelevant. He indeed demonstrated that 'absurdly strong sustainability' is in fact absurd! Let me accept that and move on to the real issue.

I did not even find the word 'complementarity' or its derivatives in the discussion, and that is the key to strong sustainability. If natural and man-made capital were substitutes (weak sustainability), then neither could be a limiting factor. If, however, they are complements (strong sustainability), then the one in short supply is limiting. Historically, in the 'empty-world' economy, man-made capital was limiting and natural capital superabundant. We have now, due to demographic and economic growth, entered the 'full-world' economy, in which the roles are reversed. More and more, the remaining natural capital now plays the role of limiting factor. The fish catch is not limited by fishing boats, but by remaining populations of fish in the sea. Economic logic says to economize on and invest in the limiting factor. For this reason we put the constraint on natural capital: maximize current welfare subject to the constraint that natural capital be maintained intact over generations.

I concur, with Beckerman not only in rejecting weak sustainability, but also in rejecting the attempt to define sustainable development in terms of the welfare of future generations. To his reasons I would only add that the welfare of future generations is beyond our control and fundamentally none of our business. As any parent knows, you cannot bequeath welfare. You can only pass on physical requirements for welfare. Nowadays natural capital is the critical requirement. A bequest of a fishing fleet with no fish left is worthless. But even the bequest of a world full of both fish and fishing boats does not guarantee welfare. Future generations are always free to make themselves miserable with whatever we leave to them. Our obligation therefore is not to guarantee their welfare, but their capacity to produce in the form of a minimum level of natural capital, the limiting factor. This can be operationalized through some simple rules of management by which human projects should be designed (constrained):

Output rule: Waste outputs are within the natural absorptive capacities of the environment (that is, non-depletion of the sink services of natural capital).
Input rules: (a) For renewable inputs, harvest rates should not exceed

regeneration rates (non-depletion of the source services of natural capital). (b) For non-renewable inputs the rate of depletion should equal the rate at which renewable substitutes can be developed. If a renewable stock is consciously divested (that is, exploited non-renewably), it should be subject to the rule for non-renewables.

Rule (b) is a 'quasi-sustainability' dictum for the exploitation of non-renewables, based on the fact that they are a capital inventory; it has been operationalized by El Serafy.[4] The question of what qualifies as a renewable substitute is relevant to the issue of strong versus weak sustainability. Weak sustainability would imply acceptance of any asset with the required rate of return. Strong sustainability requires a real rather than merely a financial substitute. For example, a capital set-aside from petroleum depletion should be invested in new energy supplies, including improvements in energy efficiency, but not in, say, more automobile factories, highways, or even medical research.

A point sure to be contested is the assertion that man-made and natural capital are complements. Many economists insist that they are substitutes. Since this is the key issue, and one that Beckerman ignores, it is necessary to repeat here the case for complementarity.

First, one way to argue is to assume the opposite and show that it is absurd. If man-made capital were a near perfect substitute for natural capital, then natural capital would be a near perfect substitute for man-made capital. But if so, there would have been no reason to accumulate man-made capital in the first place, since we humans were already endowed by nature with a near perfect substitute. But historically we did accumulate man-made capital – precisely because it is complementary to natural capital.

Second, man-made capital is itself a physical transformation of natural resources, which are the flow yield from the stock of natural capital. Therefore, producing more of the supposed substitute (man-made capital) physically requires more of the very thing being substituted for (natural capital) – the defining condition of complementarity!

Finally, man-made capital (along with labour) is an agent of transformation of the resource flow from raw material inputs into product outputs. The natural resource flow and the natural capital stock that generates it are the *material cause* of production: the capital stock that transforms raw material inputs into product outputs is the *efficient cause* of production. One cannot substitute efficient cause for material cause – as one cannot build the same wooden house with half the timber no matter how many saws and carpenters one tries to substitute. Also, to process more timber into more wooden houses, in the same time period, requires more saws, carpenters, and the like. Clearly the basic relation between man-made and natural capital is one of complementarity, not substitutability. Of course one could substitute bricks for timber, but that is the substitution of one resource input for another, not the substitution of capital for resources.[5]

The complementarity of man-made and natural capital is made obvious at a concrete and commonsense level by asking: What good is a sawmill without a forest; a fishing boat without schools of fish; a refinery without petroleum deposits; an irrigated farm without an aquifer or river? We have long recognized the complementarity between public infrastructure and private capital – what good is a car or truck without roads to drive on? Following Lotka and Georgescu-Roegen, we can take the concept of natural capital even further and distinguish between endosomatic (within-skin) and exosomatic (outside-skin) natural capital. We can then ask: What good is the private endosomatic capital of our lungs and respiratory system without the public exosomatic capital of green plants that take up our carbon dioxide in the short run, while in the long run replenishing the enormous atmospheric stock of oxygen and keeping the atmosphere at the proper mix of gases – that is, the mix to which our respiratory system is adapted and therefore complementary?

If natural and man-made capital are obviously complements, why have economists overwhelmingly treated them as substitutes? First, not all economists have – Leontief's input–output economics, with its assumption of fixed factor proportions, treats all factors as complements. Second, the formal, mathematical definitions of complementarity and substitutability are such that in the two-factor case the factors must be substitutes.[6] Since most textbooks are written on two-dimensional paper this case receives most attention. Third, mathematical convenience continues to dominate reality in the general reliance on Cobb–Douglas and other constant elasticity of substitution production functions in which there is nearly infinite substitutability of factors, in particular of capital for resources.[7] Thankfully some economists have begun to constrain this substitution by the law of conservation of mass! Fourth, exclusive myopic attention to the margin results in very limited and marginal possibilities for substitution obscuring overall relations of complementarity. For example, private expenditure on extra car maintenance may substitute for reduced public expenditure on roads. But this marginal element of substitution (car repairs for road repairs) should not obscure the fact that cars and roads are basically complementary forms of capital.[8] Fifth, there may well be substitution of capital for resources in aggregate production functions, reflecting a change in product mix from resource-intensive to capital-intensive products. But this is an artefact of changing product aggregation, not factor substitution along a given product isoquant. Also, a new product may be designed that gives the same service with less resource use – for example, light bulbs that give more lumens per watt. This is technical progress, a qualitative improvement in the state of the art, not the substitution of a quantity of capital for a quantity of resources in the production of a given quantity of a specific product.

No one denies the reality of technical progress, but to call such changes the substitution of capital for resources (or of man-made for natural capital) is a serious confusion. Some economists seem to count as 'capital' all improvements in knowledge, technology, managerial skills – in short, anything that increases the efficiency with which resources are used. If this is the usage, then 'capital' and resources would by definition be substitutes in the same sense that more efficient use of a resource is a good substitute for having more of the resource. But formally to define capital as efficiency would make a mockery of the neoclassical theory of production, where efficiency is a ratio of output to input, and capital is a quantity of input.

It was necessary here, I think, to delve deeply into the issue of complementarity because it is the key to strong sustainability, and by omitting it Beckerman failed to deal with the most important issue in the sustainable development debate.

Turning now to other problems, Beckerman thinks that discounting is the proper way to balance present and future claims on the resource base. But a discount rate is part of the price system, and prices allocate subject to a given distribution of ownership. The key question is the given distribution of ownership between different generations, which represent different people. If the resource base is thought to belong entirely to the present generation, we get one set of prices, including an interest (discount) rate. If the resource base is thought to be distributed in ownership over many generations, we get an entirely different set of prices, including a different interest rate. Both sets of prices are efficient, given the distribution.[9]

Strong sustainability as a constraint is a way of implicitly providing future generations with property rights to the resource base. It says they have ownerships claims to as much natural capital as the present generation – that is, the rule is to keep natural capital intact. This rule does not prohibit discounting; it simply establishes the condition necessary for discounting to function as a tool for allocative efficiency, namely it sets the intergenerational distribution. To allow the discount rate to determine intergenerational distribution would be totally circular because the discount rate presupposes a given intergenerational distribution of the resource base. Strong sustainability requires that man-made and natural capital each be maintained intact separately, since they are considered complements. Weak sustainability requires that only the sum of the two be maintained intact, since they are presumed to be substitutes. As natural capital more and more becomes the limiting factor, the importance of keeping it separately intact increases.

Beckerman recognizes that sustainability of consumption is built into the Hicksian definition of income (income is the maximum one can consume over some time period and still leave productive capacity, or capital, intact, so that one can produce and consume the same amount in the next period). But he downplays this respectable lineage by saying that Hicks's definition of income is a purely technical concept, containing no moral injunction against capital consumption (p. 138). While this is true in terms of accounting definitions, it is disingenuous to pretend that the prudential motive of avoiding inadvertent impoverishment by consuming beyond income played no role in Hicks's formulation of the concept. Hicksian income is a concept consciously designed to inform prudential (sustainable) consumption, even though it does not mandate it. Extending the requirement to keep capital intact to apply to natural capital as well as man-made capital is a small step, and one totally within the spirit of Hicks's prudential concerns. To the extent that natural capital is now the limiting factor, omitting it from consideration vitiates the very meaning of income and runs contrary to its prudential motivation.

In sum, I agree with Beckerman that weak sustainability is a muddle, and that definitions in terms of the welfare of future generations are non-operational. However, I have shown that strong sustainability is neither morally reprehensible nor operationally impractical, and that Beckerman's view to the contrary is based on his mistaken definition of strong sustainability. With proper definition, strong sustainability retains Beckerman's blessing as a logical constraint since it really does limit present welfare maximization and is not defined implicitly in terms of the same welfare maximization that it is supposed to limit. Strong sustainability also provides a better way of respecting the rights of future generations than does discounting. Furthermore, it represents a logical extension of the Hicksian income concept.

For all of the reasons outlined in this review, I believe that sustainable development, properly clarified (as Beckerman rightly demands), is an indispensable concept. All important concepts are dialectically vague at the margins. I claim that sustainable development is at least as clear a concept as 'money'. Is money really M1 or M2, or is it M1a? Do we count Eurodollar-based loans in the US money supply? How liquid does an asset have to be before it counts as 'quasi-money'? Yet the human mind is clever. We not only can handle the concept of money, but would have a hard time without it. The same, I suggest, is true for the concept of sustainable development.

Beckerman is a professor of economics at Oxford University and, as I mentioned earlier, an important adviser to the World Bank. He is representative of the best that orthodox academic economics has to offer. While that prestige speaks well of Beckerman's ability, it is also a poor reflection on the state of orthodox economics today. But Beckerman at least has a sense of humour, he keeps environmentalists honest, and now and again he makes some interesting points. Probably the premise of his next book will be even less stupid.

Notes

1. Parts of Beckerman's book were adapted from his essay on sustainable development in *Environmental Values*, and part of this review is adapted from my comment on his essay in the same journal: 'On Beckerman's critique of sustainable development', *Environmental Values*, **4** (1995), pp. 49–55. The US edition of Beckerman's earlier book was titled *Two Cheers for the Affluent Society* (New York: St Martin's Press, 1979).

2. For evidence that growth in GNP in the USA is no longer positively correlated with welfare increase, see Herman E. Daly and John B. Cobb, Jr, *For the Common Good* (Boston: Beacon Press, 1994), especially the Appendix on the Index of Sustainable Economic Welfare. See also Clifford W. Cobb and John B. Cobb, Jr, *The Green National Product* (New York: The University Press of America, 1994), for further criticism and discussion of the Index.

3. Donella H. Meadows, Dennis L. Meadows, and Jørgen Randers, *Beyond the Limits: Confronting Global Collapse. Envisioning a Sustainable Future* (Post Mills, VT: Chelsea Green Publishing Company, 1992).

4. Salah El Serafy, 'The proper calculation of income from depletable natural resources' in Yusuf Ahmad, Salah El Serafy and Ernst Lutz (eds), *Environmental Accounting for Sustainable Development* (Washington, DC: World Bank, 1988).

5. Regarding the house example I am frequently told that insulation (capital) is a substitute for resources (energy for space heating). If the house is considered the final product, then capital (agent of production, efficient cause) cannot end up as a part (material cause) of the house, whether as wood, brick, or insulating material. The insulating material is a resource like wood or brick, not capital. If the final product is not taken as the house but the service of the house in providing warmth, then the entire house, not only insulating material, is capital. In this case more or better capital (a well-insulated house) does reduce the waste of energy. Increasing the efficiency with which a resource is used is certainly a good substitute for more of the resource. But these kinds of waste-reducing efficiency measures (recycling prompt scrap, sweeping up sawdust and using it for fuel or particle board, reducing heat loss from a house, and so on) are all marginal substitutions that soon reach their limit.

6. The usual definition of complementarity requires that, for a given constant output, a rise in the price of one factor reduces the quantity of both factors. In the two-factor case 'both factors' means 'all factors', and it is impossible to keep output constant while reducing the input of all factors. But complementarity might be defined back into existence in the two-factor case by avoiding the constant output condition. For

example, two factors could be considered complements if an increase in one alone will not increase output, but an increase in the other will; and they might be considered perfect complements if an increase in neither factor alone will increase output, but an increase in both will. It is not sufficient to treat complementarity as if it were nothing more than 'limited substitutability'. That means we could get along well with only one factor, with the other less well, but that we do not need both. Complementarity means we need both, and that the one in shorter supply is limiting.

7.   N. Georgescu-Roegen deserves to be quoted at length on this point because so few people have understood him. He writes the 'Solow–Stiglitz variant' of the Cobb–Douglas function as:

$$Q = K^{a_1} R^{a_2} L^{a_3} \qquad (1)$$

where Q is output, K is the stock of capital, R is the flow of natural resources used in production, L is the labor supply, and $a_1 + a_2 + a_3 = 1$ and of course, $a_i > 0$.

From this formula it follows that with a constant labor power, L_0, one could obtain any Q_0, if the flow of natural resources satisfies the condition

$$R^{a_2} = \frac{Q_0}{K^{a_1} L_0^{a_3}} \qquad (2)$$

This shows that R may be as small as we wish, provided K is sufficiently large. Ergo, we can obtain a constant annual product indefinitely even from a very small stock of resources $R > 0$, if we decompose R into an infinite series $R = \Sigma R_i$ with $R_i \rightarrow 0$, use R_i in years i, and increase the stock of capital each year as required by (2). But this 'ergo' is not valid in actuality. In actuality, the increase of capital implies an additional depletion of resources. And if $K \rightarrow \infty$ then R will rapidly be exhausted by the production of capital. Solow and Stiglitz could not have come out with their conjuring trick had they borne in mind, first, that any material process consists in the transformation of some materials into others (the flow elements) by some agents (the fund elements), and second, that natural resources are the very sap of the economic process. They are not just like any other production factor. A change in capital or labor can only diminish the amount of waste in the production of a commodity; no agent can create the material on which it works. Nor can capital create the stuff out of which it is made. In some cases it may also be that the same service can be provided by a design that requires less matter or energy. But even in this direction there exists a limit, unless we believe that the ultimate fate of the economic process is an earthly Garden of Eden.

The question that confronts us today is whether we are going to discover new sources of energy that can be safely used. No elasticities of some Cobb–Douglas function can help us to answer it.

The preceding quotation is from N. Georgescu-Roegen, 'Comments on the papers by Daly and Stiglitz', in V. Kerry Smith (ed.), *Scarcity and Growth Reconsidered* (Baltimore, MD: Resources for the Future and Johns Hopkins Press, 1979), p. 98.

8.   At the margin a right glove can substitute for a left glove by turning it inside out. Socks can substitute for shoes by wearing an extra pair to compensate for thinning soles. But in spite of this marginal substitution, shoes and socks and right and left gloves are still complements. The same is true for man-made and natural capital. Picture their isoquants as L-shaped, having a 90-degree angle. Erase the angle and draw in a tiny 90-degree arc connecting the two legs of the L. This seems close to reality. However, this very marginal range of substitution has been over-extrapolated

to the degree that even a Nobel Laureate economist has gravely opined that, thanks to substitution, 'the world can, in effect, get along without natural resources' – Robert Solow, 'The economics of resources or the resources of economics', *American Economic Review* (May 1974), p. 11.

9. See R. Norgaard and R. Howarth. 'Sustainability and discounting the future', in R. Costanza (ed.), *Ecological Economics* (New York: Columbia University Press, 1991).

6   Farewell lecture to the World Bank*

After six years at the World Bank and having at 55 finally reached the age of both reason and early retirement, I am now returning to academia – to teaching, researching, writing – and chasing after grants. While I am happy about that, I also feel a sense of loss at leaving, especially because I think the Bank will become, and is already becoming, much more environmentally sensitive and literate. It is also, of all the places that I have worked, the one where I have had the best colleagues. The person who, more than anyone else, has fought for the environment in the Bank for over 15 years is Robert Goodland. Trying to help him, Salah El Serafy, and others, to 'green the Bank's economists' has been a high privilege and sometimes even fun. It is also unfinished business. The vice presidency for Environmentally Sustainable Development in its first year, under Ismail Serageldin's leadership, has been the most encouraging step forward during my time there. When the critical areas of population and energy are brought under the domain of ESD, it will be even more encouraging.

I should confess that this is a farewell from someone who is not going very far away – only nine miles up the road to the University of Maryland, so I hope to keep contact with many colleagues and with the Bank. But, who can refuse an invitation to give a farewell lecture to (take a parting shot at) such a powerful institution – an institution whose role in the world is, for better or worse, becoming ever more important, and whose imminent fiftieth birthday invites the reassessment characteristic of mid-life? I willingly succumb to the temptation both to pontificate and to prescribe a few remedies for the Bank's middle-aged infirmities.

My prescriptions will be of two kinds, internal and external. First, a few antacids and laxatives to cure the combination of managerial flatulence and organizational constipation giving rise to such a high-pressure internal environment. Second, to improve interactions with the external world, I will prescribe some new glasses and a hearing aid. After age 50 these aids to the body become more necessary and should be accepted, or at least listened to, with as much grace as possible.

* Speech delivered at the World Bank, 14 January 1994; published as chapter 9 in John Cavanagh et al. (eds), *Beyond Bretton Woods: Alternative to the global economic order*, Pluto Press, 1994, pp. 109–17.

Internal issues: the workplace and managerial environment
Many excellent people work at the World Bank, and usually work
very competently and very hard, probably too hard. But top-down
management, misguided by an unrealistic vision of development as the
generalization of Northern overconsumption to the rapidly multiplying
masses of the South, has led to many external failures, both economic
and ecological. These external failures, due to faulty vision and hearing,
will be considered later, but for now I just note that external failure
also undermines internal morale. The unrealistic vision of development
should be blamed at least as much on academic economic theorists as
on World Bank practitioners.

Management should be more open and participatory – at least managers should sometimes ask the advice of their subordinates, even if
they are not likely to take it. The Bank should be much more open –
there is really not that much to hide – or if there is I am too dumb to
see it. The Bank's failures cannot be hid for long. And it is important
not to be able to hide those things that it would be tempting to hide,
even when temporarily possible. And why one part of the Bank has to
hide things from other parts of the Bank, and especially from the
executive directors, has always puzzled me. I have even heard it said
that executive directors should be treated like cultivated mushrooms:
'kept in the dark and fed manure'. Surely that is not being open and
participatory!

Forget all this useless and unevenly applied nonsense about clearance
for speeches and published articles by professional Bank staff when they
are not officially speaking for the Bank. All that should be necessary is
a disclaimer stating clearly that the author is not speaking on behalf of
the World Bank. Of course if you *are* speaking on behalf of the Bank,
or using some kind of proprietary information, clearance is obviously
necessary. Yes, the World Bank's Administrative Manual Summary
14.20 does indeed say that disclaimers do not exempt one from submit-
ting all publications for Bank censorship because disclaimers are said
to be 'unconvincing'. But then I wonder why the Bank itself nearly
always puts a disclaimer on published Bank research? Disclaimers are
well understood – I can assure you that no one has ever mistaken a
paper of mine for a World Bank policy statement!

If some Bank office absolutely must be engaged in censoring and
'clearing' employees' non-Bank utterances, then the Bank's image is
better protected by monitoring the pretentious real estate ads of Bank
vice presidents trying to sell their expensive houses by including their
high Bank position in the description of the house, as if the prestige of
their anti-poverty office should adhere to and be capitalized in the value

of their domicile. Other worthy candidates for monitoring would be the internal memos of other vice presidents examining the 'impeccable economic logic' of dropping a given load of toxic waste on the poorest countries. Alternatively, some of that monitoring energy might be spent on controlling construction cost overruns on new Bank buildings in downtown Washington. But don't waste time trying to censor some little staff economist who, in his theoretical writings, deviates from the Bank's party line favouring free trade, NAFTA, or anything else. Fortunately, some managers are wise enough not to waste their time in this way, and my impression is that those whose duty it is to enforce clearance are very uncomfortable doing so. Without deviance there can be no change.

In sum, my internal workplace advice is: open up, loosen up, listen up, speak up and don't work weekends on anything you don't enjoy.

External issues: advice for fostering environmentally sustainable development

I have four prescriptions for better serving the goal of environmentally sustainable development through World Bank policy and action. The four prescriptions are presented in order of increasing generality and radicalism. That is, the first two are fairly specific and should, I think, be relatively non-controversial. The third will be debated by many, and the fourth will be considered outrageous by most Bank economists.

1. *Stop counting the consumption of natural capital as income.* Income is by definition the maximum amount that a society can consume this year and still be able to consume the same amount next year. That is, consumption this year, if it is to be called Income, must leave intact the capacity to produce and consume the same amount next year. Thus sustainability is built into the very definition of income. But traditionally, the productive capacity that must be maintained intact has been thought of as man-made capital only, excluding natural capital. We have habitually counted natural capital as a free good. This might have been justified in yesterday's empty world, but in today's full world it is anti-economic. The error of implicitly counting natural capital consumption as income is customary in three areas:

- the System of National Accounts (SNA);
- evaluation of projects that deplete natural capital; and
- international balance of payments accounting.

The first, SNA, is well recognized and efforts are under way to correct it – indeed, the World Bank played a pioneering role in this important initiative, and I hope will continue to contribute to 'greening the GNP'.

The second, project evaluation, is well recognized by standard economics which has long taught the need to count 'user cost' (depletion charges) as part of the opportunity cost of projects that deplete natural capital. World Bank *best* practice counts user costs, but *average* Bank practice ignores it. Uncounted user costs show up in inflated net benefits and an overstated rate of return for depleting projects. This biases investment allocation toward projects that deplete natural capital, and away from more sustainable projects.

Correcting this bias is the logical first step towards a policy of sustainable development. User cost must be counted not only for depletion of non-renewable resources, but also for projects that divest renewable natural capital by exploiting it beyond sustainable yield. The sink or absorptive services of natural capital, as well as its source or regenerative services, can also be depleted if used beyond sustainable capacity. Therefore a user cost must be charged to projects that deplete sink capacity, such as the atmosphere's ability to absorb CO_2, or the capacity of a river to carry off wastes. It is admittedly difficult to measure user cost, but attempting to avoid the issue simply means that we assign to depleted natural capital the precise default value of zero, which is frequently not the best estimate. Even when zero is the best estimate it should be arrived at not by default, but by reasoned calculation based on explicit assumptions about backstop technologies, discount rates and reserve lifetimes.

Third, in traditional balance of payments accounting the export of depleted natural capital, whether petroleum or timber cut beyond sustainable yield, is entered in the current account, and thus treated entirely as income. This is an accounting error. Some portion of those non-sustainable exports should be treated as the sale of a capital asset, and entered on capital account. If this were properly done, some countries would see their apparent balance of trade surplus converted into a true deficit, one that is being financed by drawdown and transfer abroad of their stock of natural capital. Reclassifying transactions in a way that converts a country's balance of trade from a surplus to a deficit would trigger a whole different set of IMF recommendations and actions. This reform of balance of payments accounting should be the initial focus of the IMF's new interest in environmentally sustainable development. The World Bank should warmly encourage its sister institution to get busy on this – it does not come naturally to them.

2. *Tax labour and income less, and tax resource throughput more.* In the past it has been customary for governments to subsidize resource throughput to stimulate growth. Thus energy, water, fertilizer, and even deforestation, are even now frequently subsidized. To its credit the World Bank has generally opposed these subsidies. But it is necessary to go beyond removal of explicit financial subsidies to the removal of implicit environmental subsidies as well. By 'implicit environmental subsidies' I mean external costs to the community that are not charged to the commodities whose production generates them.

Economists have long advocated internalizing external costs either by calculating and charging Pigouvian taxes (taxes which when added to marginal private costs make them equal to marginal social costs), or by Coasean redefinition of property rights (such that values that used to be public property and not valued in markets become private property whose values are protected by their new owners). These solutions are elegant in theory, but often quite difficult in practice. A blunter but much more operational instrument would be simply to shift our tax base away from labour and income on to throughput. We have to raise public revenue somehow, and the present system is highly distortionary in that by taxing labour and income in the face of high unemployment in nearly all countries, we are discouraging exactly what we want more of. The present signal to firms is to shed labour, and substitute more capital and resource throughput, to the extent feasible. It would be better to economize on throughput because of the high external costs of its associated depletion and pollution, and at the same time to use more labour because of the high social benefits associated with reducing unemployment.

Shifting the tax base to throughput induces greater throughput efficiency, and internalizes, in a gross, blunt manner, the externalities from depletion and pollution. True, the exact external costs will not have been precisely calculated and attributed to exactly those activities that caused them, as with a Pigouvian tax that aims to equate marginal social costs and benefits for each activity. But those calculations and attributions are so difficult and uncertain that insisting on them would be equivalent to a full-employment act for econometricians and prolonged unemployment and environmental degradation for everyone else. Politically the shift towards ecological taxes could be sold under the banner of revenue neutrality. However, the income tax structure should be maintained so as to keep progressivity in the overall tax structure by taxing very high incomes and subsidizing very low incomes. But the bulk of public revenue would be raised from taxes on throughput either at the depletion or pollution end.

The shift could be carried out gradually by a pre-announced schedule to minimize disruption. This shift should be a key part of structural adjustment, but should be pioneered in the North. Indeed, sustainable development itself must be achieved in the North first. It is absurd to expect any sacrifice for sustainability in the South if similar measures have not first been taken in the North. The major weakness in the World Bank's ability to foster environmentally sustainable development is that it only has leverage over the South, not the North. Some way must be found to push the North also. The Nordic countries and The Netherlands have already begun to do this.

3. *Maximize the productivity of natural capital in the short run, and invest in increasing its supply in the long run.* Economic logic requires that we behave in these two ways towards the limiting factor of production, that is maximize its productivity and invest in its increase. Those principles are not in dispute. Disagreements do exist about whether natural capital is really the limiting factor. Some argue that man-made and natural capital are such good substitutes that the very idea of a limiting factor, which requires that the factors be complementary, is irrelevant. It is true that without complementarity there is no limiting factor. So the question is, are man-made capital and natural capital basically complements or substitutes? Here again we can provide perpetual full employment for econometricians, and I would welcome more empirical work on this, even though I think it is sufficiently clear to common sense that natural and man-made capital are fundamentally complements and only marginally substitutable.

In the past natural capital has been treated as superabundant and priced at zero, so it did not really matter whether it was a complement or a substitute for man-made capital. Now remaining natural capital appears to be both scarce and complementary, and therefore limiting. For example, the fish catch is limited not by the number of fishing boats, but by the remaining populations of fish in the sea. Cut timber is limited not by the number of sawmills, but by the remaining standing forests. Pumped crude oil is limited not by man-made pumping capacity, but by remaining stocks of petroleum in the ground. The natural capital of the atmosphere's capacity to serve as a sink for CO_2 is likely to be even more limiting to the rate at which petroleum can be burned than is the source limit of remaining oil in the ground.

In the short run raising the price of natural capital by taxing throughput, as advocated above, will give the incentive to maximize natural capital productivity. Investing in natural capital over the long run is also needed. But how do we invest in something which by definition we cannot make? If we could make it, it would be man-made capital! For renewable resources we have the possibility of fallowing investments, or more generally 'waiting' in the Marshallian sense – allowing this year's growth increment to be added to next year's growing stock rather than consuming it. For non-renewables we do not have this option. We can only liquidate them. So the question is how fast do we liquidate, and how much of the proceeds can we count as income if we invest the rest in the best available renewable substitute? And, of course, how much of the correctly counted income do we then consume and how much do we invest?

One renewable substitute for natural capital is the mixture of natural and man-made capital represented by plantations and fish farms, which we may call 'cultivated natural capital'. But even within this important hybrid category we have a complementary combination of natural and man-made capital components. For example, a plantation forest may use man-made capital to plant trees, control pests and choose the proper rotation – but the complementary natural capital services of rainfall, sunlight and soil are still there, and eventually still become limiting. Also, cultivated natural capital usually requires a reduction in biodiversity relative to natural capital proper.

For both renewable and non-renewable resources, investments in enhancing throughput productivity are needed. Increasing resource productivity is indeed a good substitute for finding more of the resource. But the main point is that investment should be in the limiting factor, and to the extent that natural capital has replaced man-made capital as the limiting factor, the Bank's investment focus should shift correspondingly. I do not believe that it has. In fact, the failure to charge user cost on natural capital depletion, noted earlier, surely biases investment away from replenishing projects.

4. *Move away from the ideology of global economic integration by free trade, free capital mobility and export-led growth – and towards a more nationalist orientation that seeks to develop domestic production for internal markets as the first option, having recourse to international trade only when clearly much more efficient.* At the present time global interdependence is celebrated as a self-evident good. The royal road to development, peace and harmony is thought to be the unrelenting conquest of each nation's market by all other nations. The word 'globalist' has politically correct connotations, while the word 'nationalist' has come to be pejorative. This is so much the case that it is necessary to remind ourselves that the World Bank exists to serve the interests of its members, which are nation states, national communities – not

individuals, not corporations, not even NGOs. It has no charter to serve the one-world-without-borders cosmopolitan vision of global integration, nor to convert many relatively independent national economies, loosely dependent on international trade, into one tightly integrated world economic network upon which the weakened nations depend for even basic survival.

The model of international community upon which the Bretton Woods institutions rests is that of a 'community of communities', an international federation of *national* communities cooperating to solve global problems under the principle of subsidiarity. The model is not the cosmopolitan one of direct global citizenship in a single integrated world community without intermediation by nation states.

To globalize the economy by erasure of national economic boundaries through free trade, free capital mobility, and free or at least uncontrolled migration is to wound fatally the major unit of community capable of carrying out any policies for the common good. That includes not only national policies for purely domestic ends, but also international agreements required to deal with those environmental problems that are irreducibly global (such as CO_2 and ozone depletion). International agreements presuppose the ability of national governments to carry out policies in their support. If nations have no control over their borders, they are in a poor position to enforce national laws, including those necessary to secure compliance with international treaties.

Cosmopolitan globalism weakens national boundaries and the power of national and subnational communities, while strengthening the relative power of transnational corporations. Since there is no world government capable of regulating global capital in the global interest, and since the desirability and possibility of a world government are both highly doubtful, it will be necessary to make capital less global and more national. I know that is an unthinkable thought right now, but take it as a prediction – ten years from now the buzz words will be 'renationalization of capital' and the 'community rooting of capital for the development of national and local economies', not the current shibboleths of export-led growth stimulated by whatever adjustments are necessary to increase global competitiveness. 'Global competitiveness' (frequently a thought-substituting slogan) usually reflects not so much a real increase in resource productivity as a standards-lowering competition to reduce wages, externalize environmental and social costs, and export natural capital at low prices while calling it income.

The World Bank should use the occasion of its fiftieth birthday to reflect deeply on the forgotten words of one of its founders, John Maynard Keynes:

> I sympathize therefore, with those who would minimize, rather than those who would maximize, economic entanglement between nations. Ideas, knowledge, art, hospitality, travel – these are the things which should of their nature be international. But let goods be homespun whenever it is reasonably and conveniently possible; and, above all, let finance be primarily national.

7 Review of Martin W. Lewis's *Green Delusions: an environmentalist critique of radical environmentalism* (Duke University Press, 1992)*

Former Texas Commissioner of Agriculture, Jim Hightower, when asked why his political views were not more safely middle of the road, replied, 'There ain't nothing in the middle of the road but a yellow stripe and dead armadillos'. Well, there is one other thing – Professor Martin Lewis. Mr Lewis walks down that yellow stripe, stepping over the dead armadillos, and throwing stones at any eco-creature, living or moribund, that is too far to the right or left of dead centre. Sometimes his stones are well aimed and the miserably eccentric eco-parasite gets what it deserves. But often Lewis's aim is erratic. In a world full of polarities and tensions, the middle of the road is usually a safe place to be, although an autopsy on some of the dead armadillos might have revealed otherwise.

My annoyance at Lewis's oppressive moderation had grown intense by page 177, when it was defused by the disarming personal comment that he had been 'an undergraduate at University of California, Santa Cruz, where marxist, primitivist, and anarchistic philosophies prevailed', and where students stopped playing sports in a competitive manner so as to spare the egos of the less-skilled players. From such a politically correct beginning, any subsequent reversion to mainstreamism had to be viewed sympathetically.

The book is about anti-human anarchism, primitivism, humanist eco-anarchism, eco-marxism, and eco-feminism (p. 27). If you are thirsting for rambling, preachy dissertations on these topics, with asides on free market environmentalism, neo luddism, Third World development and population – then this is the book for you. Lewis's thesis is that these radicals are all sloppy thinkers whose Arcadian delusions give main-stream Promethean Environmentalists, like himself, an undeserved bad name, and make their message politically more difficult to sell. There is certainly some truth to this, and eco-freaks really should thank Lewis for taking them seriously enough to try to correct their errors, especially

* Published in *Ecological Economics*, **9** (2), February 1994. The views here expressed are those of the reviewer, and should in no way be attributed to the World Bank.

since no one else does,[1] at least outside Santa Cruz where, instead of honest criticism, all they get is non-competitive ego reinforcement.

Although I was not vitally interested in the exhaustive taxonomy of eco-radicalisms, I was very interested to learn what was the common feature that separated the deluded radical Arcadian environmentalists from those clear-eyed Prometheans sitting on the yellow stripe. Lewis is not only explicit, but emphatic, in his answer. The root of all green delusion is the acceptance of the necessity of a steady-state economy.

It would be idle for me to pretend that my interest in his answer was not piqued by reference to my own work as a major source of this foundational delusion. However, the following quote clearly shows the critical importance that the author himself attributes to this 'fundamental point'. The emphasis is such as would have demanded the attention of even the unindicted reviewer.

> Ultimately, green extremism is rooted in a single, powerful conviction: that continued economic growth is absolutely impossible, given the limits of the finite planet. Only if this notion is discredited can the edifice of eco-radical philosophy be shaken.
>
>   It can logically be shown that the supposed necessity of devising a steady-state economy is severely misconstrued. (p. 10)

I was eager to peruse what would surely be a careful argument against this ultimate root of all radical eco-philosophy from an author whose central purpose is to discredit it. Will this argument take the rest of the book? A chapter? To my amazement it takes only half a page in the Introduction! Here it is: 'Economic growth, strictly speaking, is defined as an increase in the *value* of goods *and* services' (his emphasis). Since value is not the same as mass, and since services are non-consumptive, we can do an end run around limits stemming from the physical finitude of the planet and have economic growth for ever. Therefore steady-state economics is wrong.

But slow down, please, Mr Lewis. Value, in the context of economic growth, does not refer to pixie dust. It means a sum of money equal to price times quantity of commodities. To measure economic growth (growth in real GNP) we hold prices constant so that change in value will come only from change in quantity of the commodities. Quantities of goods *and* services have a physical dimension (mass and energy), and are therefore subject to physical laws of conservation and entropy. Economic value is certainly not reducible to physical laws, but neither is it exempt from them. Real GNP is a value index of quantitative change. The creation of a value index to measure aggregate quantitative change in output does *not* annihilate the physical dimensions of commodities, thereby allowing the economy to grow for ever on a finite planet!!

Mr Lewis could clear his mind of the brown delusion that services are physically non-consumptive by just taking a good look at the physical plant of George Washington University, especially the hospital, where services of education and medical care are daily produced all around him. The idea that economic growth, even the growth of a service institution like GWU, can continue for ever because it can be decoupled from matter and energy is angelistic nonsense. Lewis's claim that the case for a steady-state economy is discredited because it is 'one that largely ignores services and substitutes mass for value' is to carry confusion to the point of misrepresentation.

Evidently realizing that he has veered from the middle of the road, Lewis begins to retreat in the next paragraph. He grants that 'the more sophisticated advocates of a steady-state economy' do in fact distinguish quantitative from qualitative growth, and that only the former must at some point be constrained by physical finitude. The latter is free to improve ('grow qualitatively') within the physical constraint of the former. But he still thinks services belong only to the qualitative category ('nonconsumptive forms of economic growth', he calls them), and chides me for not recognizing this, although I discussed the question extensively in the very reference he cites.

In the following paragraph we get the further concession that services, after all, do require physical maintenance, and the argument then shifts to the possibility of 'dematerialization', which evidently means nothing more than 'expanding in value by producing better goods and services more efficiently', which is nothing other than the 'qualitative improvement' not only recognized but advocated by the steady-state view. Indeed, the steady-state policy is to redirect the path of progress entirely to qualitative improvement by closing off the alternative path of quantitative expansion. Nor does Lewis seem to recognize that qualitative improvements frequently do not register as growth in measured value. This does not mean that such improvements are not desirable, but that they increase uncounted consumer surplus rather than expenditure and measured value. All good things do not necessarily increase economic growth, and all increases in economic growth are not necessarily good things.

Lewis believes that economic growth is always to the good and thinks environmentalists are obtuse not to see this.

Whereas moderate environmentalists see some benefit to economic growth (a more prosperous society being able to afford more environmental protection) green stalwarts consider this proposition self-cancelling. (pp. 3–4)

The problem with Lewis's statement is that it identifies greater prosperity (a state) with economic growth (a process supposedly leading to that state). No one denies that if we were truly richer or more prosperous all our problems, including environmental protection, would be easier to solve. But the question at issue is: Does economic growth, as currently measured from the existing margin, really make us richer? Might it not be making us poorer by increasing environmental costs faster than production benefits? If the latter were the case, how would we recognize it? Not by looking at GNP, because it includes the expenditure incurred to protect ourselves against the unwanted environmental costs, and thus registers as a further increase in economic growth. And Lewis thinks that must make us richer!

In sum, Lewis has not refuted the argument for a steady-state economy which he says is the basis of all the radicalisms that the rest of his book is dedicated to criticizing. But that task is not as fundamental to the rest of his book as he thinks, so his failure to accomplish it is really not very damaging to his other criticisms. This is because, contrary to Lewis's assertion, it is just not true that eco-marxists, eco-feminists, eco-anarchists and the like all begin their analyses by accepting the necessity of the steady-state economy, and found their arguments on that premise. My experience is that most of these eco-parasites have never heard of steady-state economics, and even if they have it does not matter because they do not understand it any better than Lewis does.

Lewis is ungenerous in presenting the views of others. Wendell Berry, for example, reasonably suggests that the modern world has a lot to learn about farming from the Amish. Lewis counters that Amish success in farming is due to their numerous children and implies that Berry would turn the USA into Bangladesh by advocating that our farmers adopt an Amish way of life (p. 145). It is certainly fair to point out that not all features of the Amish way of life are good for the environment. But might it not be possible to learn something from Amish farming practices without adopting their fertility behaviour – or their dress or music, or the entire Amish way of life? This is unfair and ungenerous treatment of Berry, who did not advocate the adoption of the Amish way of life, but only said that we could learn something from their agricultural practices. After all, any group that can make a good living from small farms for a century without government aid and without mining the soil might be doing something right.

Worse treatment is given to Paul and Anne Ehrlich. Lewis criticizes their use of the I=PAT identity (impact on environment equals population times affluence times technology – a rather popularized way of stating an important relationship), claiming that they are guilty of multiplying non-quantities together (p. 238) and of reducing environmental impact to a unitary phenomenon. Further, Lewis claims that this extraordinarily useful and unpretentious identity is 'an example of pseudo-science, impressive only to those mystified by equations and other scholarly trappings'. Actually Lewis is the one mystified by the equation, since he incredibly interprets it to mean that 'every advance in pollution control technology would contribute to the population explosion' (p. 238). In Lewis's defence, the popular source he cites did not explain the logic underlying the formula nor demonstrate just what it means and does not mean. It took that knowledge for granted. But the Ehrlichs provided references to earlier scholarly works in which the identity was fully explained and developed. Lewis owed it to the reader, and to the Ehrlichs, to follow up those references and educate himself before making such absurd and intemperate accusations.

In marine ecology certain fish perform the function of cleaning the parasites off of other fish. When a fish is ready to be cleaned it assumes a vertical position, a signal to the cleaner fish to come and get a free meal by eating its parasites. There are a lot of intellectual and ideological parasites (eco-anarchists, eco-marxists, eco-feminists, eco-free marketists . . .) that seek to re-energize their flagging vigour by hyphenating themselves with ecology or environmentalism. Lewis has performed a sometimes valuable cleaning service, and for that deserves credit. There are also other fish that mimic the cleaner fish in order to get close enough to take a bite out of the hapless fish being cleaned. Lewis has also played that game, and on that score deserves to be bitten back.

Note
1. As Lewis himself notes, 'Eco-radicalism is admittedly a marginal social movement, its adherents forming an exiguous ideological minority' (p. 247).

III   On economists' misunderstanding of thermodynamics

Introduction

Chapters 11 and 12 are early attempts in standard journals politely to correct economists' misunderstandings of the relevance of the entropy law to economics, especially as that relevance had been expounded by Georgescu-Roegen. Since these attempts seemed to get nowhere, I decided to be more aggressive. The result was the challenge set forth in Chapters 8 and 9, put first here because they are also more expository. They are part of a symposium on Georgescu-Roegen's contribution to ecological economics (*Ecological Economics*, September 1997). Such a symposium seemed an opportune time to revive Georgescu-Roegen's unanswered criticism of neoclassical production theory, specifically as employed by Robert Solow and Joseph Stiglitz. These two very prominent economists were invited to reply to the criticisms that Georgescu-Roegen had made of their work twenty years ago. One of the economists (Robert Solow) had received the Nobel prize for the work under criticism, so he was not without support from the establishment in ignoring Georgescu-Roegen's critique. After twenty years of stonewalling by Solow and Stiglitz, during which time Georgescu-Roegen died, we finally got a reply. I invite the reader to judge whether or not Solow's reply is adequate. Chapter 10 elaborates the critique of neoclassical production theory and sketches a more promising alternative.

8 Georgescu-Roegen versus Solow/ Stiglitz*

In his Richard T. Ely Lecture to the American Economics Association, Robert Solow (Solow, 1974, p. 11) stated that 'If it is very easy to substitute other factors for natural resources, then there is in principle no "problem". The world can, in effect, get along without natural resources . . .' As an 'if – then' statement, this is no less true than saying, 'If wishes were horses then beggars would ride.' But the facts are that wishes are not horses, and that natural resources and capital are generally not substitutes, but complements. While it is no doubt useful to state this conditional possibility for the sake of logical completeness in cataloguing alternatives, one would expect that the production-without-resources case, once recognized, would be quickly set aside as unrealistic and unworthy of further analysis. However, Solow does not set it aside, but retains it as a real possibility. In fact, it is precisely this 'real possibility' that has provided the foundation for a significant part of his previous work. His well-known work in growth theory is based on an aggregate production function in which resources do not appear at all, and which takes production to be a function only of capital and labour. That production function is a mathematically clear way of saying that 'the world can, in effect, get along without natural resources'.

What evidence does Solow offer for this remarkable affirmation about the way the world works? In the next paragraph he says, 'Fortunately, what little evidence there is suggests that there is quite a lot of substitutability between exhaustible resources and renewable or reproducible resources . . .' True enough, but irrelevant. The issue is not substitution between two types of natural resource; rather it is one of substitution of capital for resources, an entirely different matter. Easy substitution between two types of natural resource will not help the world to get along without natural resources!

Since the production function is often explained as a technical recipe, we might say that Solow's recipe calls for making a cake with only the cook and his kitchen. We do not need flour, eggs, sugar, and so on, nor electricity or natural gas, nor even firewood. If we want a bigger cake, the cook simply stirs faster in a bigger bowl and cooks the empty bowl

* Published in *Ecological Economics*, **22** (3), September 1997, pp. 261–6.

in a bigger oven that somehow heats itself. Nor does the cook have any cleaning up to do, because the production recipe produces no wastes. There are no rinds, peelings, husks, shells or residues, nor is there any waste heat from the oven to be vented. Furthermore, we can make not only a cake, but any kind of dish – a gumbo, fried chicken, a paella, bananas foster, cherries jubilee – all without worrying about the qualitatively different ingredients, or even about the quantity of any ingredient at all! Real recipes in real cookbooks, by contrast, *begin* with a list of specific ingredients and amounts.

A technical production recipe that contradicts both the first and second laws of thermodynamics, as well as best practice in cooking, is more than a little troubling. It led Georgescu-Roegen to the following verdict on Solow:

> One must have a very erroneous view of the economic process as a whole not to see that there are no material factors other than natural resources. To maintain further that 'the world can, in effect, get along without natural resources' is to ignore the difference between the actual world and the Garden of Eden. (Georgescu-Roegen, 1975, p. 361)

Perhaps as an unacknowledged concession to Georgescu-Roegen's criticism, we find some years later a new version of the production function in which resources appear along with labour and capital, all multiplied together in a Cobb–Douglas function. Georgescu-Roegen labelled this the 'Solow–Stiglitz variant', and showed that including R (resources) in this type of production function simply sweeps the contradiction under the rug, without removing it.

Georgescu-Roegen deserves to be quoted at length on this point. He writes the 'Solow–Stiglitz variant' of the Cobb–Douglas function as:

$$Q = K^{a_1} R^{a_2} L^{a_3} \qquad (1)$$

where Q is output, K is the stock of capital, R is the flow of natural resources used in production, L is the labor supply, and $a_1 + a_2 + a_3 = 1$ and of course, $a_i > 0$. From this formula it follows that with a constant labor power, L_0, one could obtain any Q_0, if the flow of natural resources satisfies the condition

$$R^{a_2} = \frac{Q_0}{K^{a_1} L_0^{a_3}} \qquad (2)$$

This shows that R may be as small as we wish, provided K is sufficiently large. Ergo, we can obtain a constant annual product indefinitely even from a very small stock of resources $R > 0$, if we decompose R into an infinite series $R = \Sigma R_i$, with $R_i \rightarrow 0$, use R_i in year i, and increase the stock of capital each year as required by (2). But this 'ergo' is not valid in actuality. In actuality, the increase of capital implies an additional depletion of resources. And if $K \rightarrow \infty$, then R will rapidly be exhausted by the production of capital. Solow and Stiglitz could not have come out with their conjuring trick had they borne in mind, first, that any material process consists in the transformation of some materials into others (the flow elements) by some agents (the fund elements), and second, that natural resources are the very sap of the economic process. They are not just like any other production factor. A change in capital or labor can only diminish the amount of waste in the production of a commodity: no agent can create the material on which it works. Nor can capital create the stuff out of which it is made. In some cases it may also be that the same service can be provided by a design that requires less matter or energy. But even in this direction there exists a limit, unless we believe that the ultimate fate of the economic process is an earthly Garden of Eden. The question that confronts us today is whether we are going to discover new sources of energy that can be safely used. No elasticities of some Cobb–Douglas function can help us to answer it. (Georgescu-Roegen, 1979, p. 98) (See also Stiglitz, 1979, p. 41, fn 5)

To my knowledge neither Solow nor Stiglitz has ever replied to Georgescu-Roegen's critique. What reply could they make? Let us consider a few possibilities that others have put forward in similar contexts.

First, it might be argued that resources can be left out of the production function because they are not really scarce. Air is usually necessary for production, but we do not explicitly enter it in the function because it is considered a free good. This argument loses plausibility as soon as we remember that most resources are not free goods. Furthermore, we cannot logically use price, even a zero price, as a coefficient of factors in the production function. The production function is a technical recipe with all terms in physical units, not value units.[1] The fact that *aggregate* production functions must use prices as weights in calculating an aggregate quantity index (dollar's worth) of capital (or labour or resources) is a fundamental problem that limits the usefulness of aggregate production functions, not an answer to the difficulty just raised. Also, expressing the quantities of different factors in units of the same numeraire reflects an assumption, not a demonstration, that the factors are substitutes.

Second, it is sometimes argued that leaving resources out of the production function is justified by the implicit assumption that resources can be perfectly substituted by reproducible capital. Nordhaus and Tobin (1972) are quite explicit:

The prevailing standard model of growth assumes that there are no limits on the feasibility of expanding the supplies of nonhuman agents of production. It is basically a two-factor model in which production depends only on labor and reproducible capital. Land and resources, the third member of the classical triad, have generally been dropped ... the tacit justification has been that reproducible capital is a near perfect substitute for land and other exhaustible resources.

If that were the case then we could equally well leave out capital and include natural resources (substitution is reversible), yet no one suggests doing that (for related discussion, see Victor, 1991). To do that would run counter to the whole animus of neoclassical theory, which is to deny any important role to nature.[2]

The Solow–Stiglitz variant includes resources explicitly, but implicitly makes a similar assumption about near perfect substitution of capital for resources – what Georgescu-Roegen aptly dismissed as a 'conjuring trick'. In the Solow–Stiglitz variant, to make a cake we need not only the cook and his kitchen, but also some non-zero amount of flour, sugar, eggs, and so on. This seems a great step forward until we realize that we could make our cake a thousand times bigger with no extra ingredients, if we simply stirred faster and used bigger bowls and ovens. The conjuring trick is to give the appearance of respecting the first law of thermodynamics (material balance) without really doing so.

Another argument for the unimportance of resources was offered in the influential book *Scarcity and Growth* (Barnett and Morse, 1963, p. 11), where it was argued that

Advances in fundamental science have made it possible to take advantage of the uniformity of matter/energy, a uniformity that makes it feasible without preassignable limit, to escape the quantitative constraints imposed by the character of the earth's crust ... Nature imposes particular scarcities, not an inescapable general scarcity.

Just below the surface lies the alchemist's dream of converting lead into gold. All we need from nature are uniform, indestructible building blocks – the alchemical 'quintessence' or 'fifth essence' to which the traditional four essences (earth, air, fire and water) are thought to be reducible, and through which they become convertible one into the other. Given the building blocks, all the rest is transmutation – value added by capital and labour (and perhaps a few magic words or symbols). Technical improvement enables labour and capital to add more value to the inert building blocks, but nature remains unnecessary beyond the initial provision of those blocks. This view at least respects the first law of thermodynamics, but unfortunately crashes headlong into the second law. While it may be technically possible to convert lead into gold, thereby eliminating the particular scarcity of gold, we do not thereby remove general scarcity, because the potential for making such conversions is itself scarce. That potential must be continually used up by the economy and resupplied by nature in the form of low-entropy natural resources.

Another possible reply would be to take off from Georgescu-Roegen's qualification that in some cases 'the same service may be provided by a design that requires less matter or energy'. This implicitly introduces a distinction between substitution among factors within a given set of technologies (existing state of the art), and substitution among factors made possible by a new technology (improved state of the art). Even the latter case is limited. Future technologies must also conform to the laws of thermodynamics, Georgescu-Roegen insists, but he leaves it at that. Just how far new technology can ease the burden of scarcity, within the constraint of physical laws, remains an open question. But that really is another subject from the one at hand, since in constructing their aggregate production function Solow/Stiglitz aim to represent actual production processes of today and the recent past – not unknown future possibilities. It is as an empirically based representation of actual production processes that their production function is intended, and it is as such that it fails. That it would also fail to depict future technologies is an *a fortiori* criticism.

In an article otherwise critical of neoclassical theory, Ayres (Ayres, 1996, p. 12) offers a last-ditch defence of Solow–Stiglitz, in the absence of which he considers Georgescu-Roegen's critique 'devastating'. Ayres's too-generous defence is that 'in the distant future the economic system need not produce significant amounts of material goods at all'. Further down the same page he implicitly conflates the production function with the utility function to make the claim that 'nobody can define a finite absolute minimum material input required to produce a unit of economic welfare'. Maybe not, but we were talking about physical output, not welfare. Even production functions that yield services are producing a physical output – the use of some*thing* or some*body* for some period of time. That is different from utility or welfare. The service of my physician may not increase my welfare at all, and could even reduce it, but it remains a measurable service for which I am charged. But even without this clarification Ayres found it necessary immediately to condition his statement, questioning the existence of a minimum material input, by adding 'with the obvious exception of food and drink'. Are there not other obvious exceptions, such as clothing and shelter?

Maybe there are other replies to Georgescu-Roegen's criticism that are less unconvincing than those considered above, but if so then Solow or Stiglitz should break their silence and finally reply to Georgescu-Roegen's criticism of long standing. Of course Georgescu-Roegen is now deceased, but his critique did not die with him. Serious criticism and serious replies are both essential parts of science. When a fundamental critique from a very prominent economist goes for twenty years without a reply, we should worry about the health of our discipline!

Consider a further major difficulty resulting from the conjuring trick of just plugging R into a production function along with K and L. An immediate consequence is that the marginal physical products of K and L would have to be zero once R is included in the function. This is because the definition of marginal product of one factor requires that the amounts of all other factors be held constant as one more unit of the variable factor is added. But when resources are held constant, there can be no extra unit of output as labour or capital is increased because there is no extra physical substance for the extra output to be made from. It would have to be produced out of nothing, again fracturing the first law of thermodynamics.[3] The point of course is not limited to Cobb–Douglas functions – any production function that obeys the first law of thermodynamics cannot avoid a strict complementarity between resources on the one hand and capital or labour on the other hand.[4]

Zero marginal physical products of labour and capital, a necessary consequence of including R in any production function that obeys the most basic laws of nature, would destroy neoclassical distribution theory – perhaps too heavy a price to pay for admission that the world, in effect, *cannot* get along without natural resources! And once we admit that natural processes, as well as labour and capital, add value to the indestructible building blocks, then we must ask who has the right to appropriate nature's contribution. These are not trivial issues! Of course, we can continue to write mathematical functions that contradict physical laws, call them 'production' functions, take the partial derivatives of L and K, and still label them marginal products of labour and capital. But then, as Georgescu-Roegen put it, this becomes a 'mere paper-and-pencil operation' (PAP was his acronym).

Georgescu's fund-flow model of the production process is superior to the neoclassical production function. It emphasizes that physically what we call 'production' is really transformation – of resources into useful products and waste products. Labour and capital are agents of transformation (efficient causes), while resources, low-entropy matter/energy, are 'that which is being transformed' (material causes). We can often substitute one efficient cause for another, or one material cause for another, but the relation between efficient and material cause is fundamentally one of complementarity, not substitutability.

If we wish to retain the neoclassical production function then we must at least include natural resource inputs and waste outputs, and must adopt mathematical representations that, unlike the customary multiplicative forms, do not assume that agents of transformation (funds) can substitute for the resources undergoing transformation (flows). Accuracy of analytical representation of reality must replace mathematical tractability as the main criterion of a good model. Once we recognize the reality of inputs from nature then we must inquire about their scarcity and about the ecological processes that regenerate them. Once we recognize the necessity of returning waste outputs to nature then we must inquire about the capacities of ecosystems to absorb those wastes. We will no longer be able to avoid the ecological economist's vision of the economy as an open subsystem of a complex ecosystem that is finite, non-growing, and materially closed. In effect, neoclassical economists will become ecological economists!

Toward that happy end it is appropriate to reissue Georgescu-Roegen's invitation to Solow/Stiglitz, and the whole community of neo-classical economists for whom they are distinguished spokesmen, to put an end to 'conjuring tricks' – to mathematical fun and games with infinity in the Garden of Eden – and to devote their impressive analytical powers to helping develop serious ecological economics for the real world.[5]

Acknowledgements
For helpful comments on earlier drafts I am grateful to R. Ayres, S. El Serafy, J. Gowdy, B. Hannon, G. Lozada, R. Nelson, T. Page and P. Victor. Of course, remaining shortcomings are mine alone.

Notes
1. To see why this must be so, recall the following chain of derivations. From the production function we derive the cost function by introducing factor prices, and from the cost function we derive the supply curve by introducing a schedule of product prices. From the utility function we derive the demand curve with the aid of an introduced schedule of product prices. The interaction of supply and demand simultaneously determines equilibrium prices and quantities. If we already have those prices included in either the production or utility functions, then we are assuming from the beginning that which is ultimately to be explained. Simultaneous determination by supply and demand is one thing, but circular reasoning is something else.
2. Acceptance of the dogma that nature makes no contribution to production allows some neoclassical economists to assume that any increase in production not explained by increases in labour or capital must be the result of some other humanly created factor, namely technology. Such economists do not flinch from claiming that a 50 per

cent unexplained residual must really be a measure of technological progress (human ingenuity). In fact the residual is a measure of everything that is not labour and capital, including, of course, natural resources. To make matters worse, as Georgescu-Roegen pointed out, capital and labour themselves have a necessary and significant resource content from which neoclassical production functions totally abstract.

3. The aggregate production function is taken to be in physical units, as in microeconomics. The aggregate production functions of macroeconomics may seem to be in value units because prices are used to aggregate the variables, but fundamentally a 'dollar's worth' of capital, labour or resources is a physical quantity. The relationship expressed by the function is a relationship among physical quantities, not values. By expressing physical quantities as 'dollar's worth' we do not escape the physical laws of mass balance and entropy!

4. It is unavailing to appeal to the alternative definition of marginal product as the decline in total product resulting from using one less unit of the variable factor, because R still has to be constant, and if we use one unit less of capital or labour then we will have some R left unneeded. But to keep R constant we must use the unneeded amount anyway, that is, use it wastefully. That means the function is not a technically efficient recipe and therefore does not qualify as a relevant production function.

5. A perceptive reviewer suggested that the best way to get an answer to Georgescu-Roegen's critique is probably not to raise it again with the same people that have ignored it for twenty years, but rather to somehow get 10 000 students to ask their economics professors the following questions in class: (1) Do you believe that economic activities must satisfy mass balance? (2) Why is it that neoclassical production functions do not satisfy the condition of mass balance? (3) Do you believe that Georgescu-Roegen's interpretation of production as physical transformation is correct? (4) Do you agree that the economic system is embedded in the larger environmental system, and totally dependent on it as both source and sink for the matter/energy transformed by economic activity? (5) Do you believe that the matter/energy transformations required by economic activity are constrained by the entropy law? Ten thousand students, please take note!

References

Ayres, R.U. (1996), 'Theories of Economic Growth', INSEAD, Fontainebleau, France, September.

Barnett, Harold and Chandler, Morse (1963), *Scarcity and Growth*, Baltimore, MD: RFF and Johns Hopkins Press.

Georgescu-Roegen, Nicholas (1975), 'Energy and economic myths', *Southern Economic Journal*, **XLI** (3), January 1975, 347–81.

Georgescu-Roegen, Nicholas (1979), 'Comments on the papers by Daly and Stiglitz', in Smith, V. Kerry (ed.), *Scarcity and Growth Reconsidered*, Baltimore, MD: RFF and Johns Hopkins Press.

Nordhaus, William and Tobin, James (1972), *Economic Growth*, New York: National Bureau of Economic Research Columbia University Press.

Solow, Robert (1974), 'The economics of resources or the resources of economics', *American Economic Review*, **64** (2), May 1974, 1–14.

Stiglitz, J.E. (1979), 'A Neoclassical Analysis of the Economics of Natural Resources', in Smith, V. Kerry (ed.), *Scarcity and Growth Reconsidered*, Baltimore, MD: RFF and Johns Hopkins Press.

Victor, P.A. (1991), 'Indicators of sustainable development: Some lessons from capital theory', *Ecological Economics*, **4**, 191–213.

9   Reply to Solow/Stiglitz*

Criticism and response are both necessary to science. That is why I thought it worthwhile to revive Georgescu-Roegen's critique of neoclassical production theory, and why the editors of *Ecological Economics* invited replies from Solow and Stiglitz, whom Georgescu-Roegen took as leading representatives of the body of thought that he was criticizing. I am grateful to Solow and Stiglitz for taking the time to reply.

Curiously, neither of their replies even mentioned Georgescu-Roegen. That in itself would not be so bad had their comments been responsive to the criticisms that Georgescu-Roegen raised twenty years ago, and that I restated. But both Solow and Stiglitz chose, for the most part, simply to repeat their well-known position, rather than to engage Georgescu-Roegen's arguments against their position. I say 'for the most part' because, in closing, Solow did respond directly, albeit briefly, to the five questions raised in my note 5. Since this seems a promising basis for further dialogue I will repeat the five questions and Solow's answers, followed by my comment on each. But first a word on Stiglitz.

Georgescu-Roegen did not misunderstand the intermediate-run nature of the questions that Stiglitz claims are the focus of the models under discussion. Georgescu-Roegen considered the 50-year time frame critical because that is the period in which we will have to shift our dependence from terrestrial to solar low entropy, as fossil fuels are depleted. His point was not that the neoclassical model of production is 'as if' in the way that all models are, but rather that it so badly misrepresents the process of production (see following discussion of the five questions) that it cannot shed any light on this critical transition. A reply to that criticism would be interesting. Nevertheless, Stiglitz's recognition of limits to population growth constitutes a real advance within the neoclassical framework. Building on this insight, perhaps the World Bank, under his leadership, will investigate whether limits to the growth of the population of human bodies might have some analogues in limits to growth of the populations of cars, of houses, of refrigerators, of cattle, and so on. The aggregate population of all these dissipative structures (things that require an entropic throughput for

* Published in *Ecological Economics*, **22** (3), September 1997, pp. 271–3.

their maintenance) is a concept very relevant to ecological economics, and worthy of the World Bank's investigation.

Let us turn now to the five questions from note 5, and a consideration of Solow's answers:

1. Do you believe that economic activities must satisfy mass balance?
Solow's answer: 'Yes'.
Comment.   Agreed.

2. Why is it that neoclassical production functions do not satisfy the condition of mass balance?
Solow's answer: 'Because up until now, and at the level of aggregation, geographic scope and temporal extent considered, mass balance has not been a controlling factor in the growth of industrial economies.'
Comment: Mass balance holds at all levels of aggregation, geographic scope, and temporal extent – so Solow's qualifications seem beside the point. I think what Solow means is that material balance is unimportant because materials themselves are unimportant, which is implied by his use of a production function in which material flows are either absent or somehow substitutable by capital stocks. If material flows themselves are not important, then material balances would not be important either. That is why Georgescu-Roegen criticized Solow for analysing 'the Garden of Eden' rather than the real world. The criticism remains unanswered. Does the qualification 'up until now' indicate an expectation that the situation is about to change, that the mass balance constraint is gaining relevance?

3. Do you believe that Georgescu-Roegen's interpretation of production as physical transformation is correct?
Solow's answer: 'This is no doubt one aspect of production.'
Comment: Yes, but Solow has treated it as a very unimportant aspect – one that could safely be abstracted from in the analytical representation of production. Georgescu-Roegen criticized him for that – for abstracting from the essential, rather than from the incidental. If production is essentially the transformation of a flow of resource inputs into product outputs, with capital and labour funds serving as agents of transformation, then capital and resources must be more in the nature of complements than substitutes. As Georgescu-Roegen noted, agents of transformation cannot create the materials they transform, nor the materials out of which the agents themselves are made. Agents of transformation and material undergoing transformation are basically complements – they can be substitutes only along the margin of reducing

waste of materials-in-process to zero – for example using a press to make particle board out of wood chips and sawdust. But then the press (capital) and the wood chips (resources) are again complements. Solow makes no recognition at all of this fundamental complementarity. Complementarity is pushed further offstage by its more technical definition based on constant output (which rules complementarity out of existence in a two-factor world). Georgescu-Roegen remains unanswered.

4. Do you agree that the economic system is embedded in the larger environmental system, and totally dependent on it as both source and sink for the matter/energy transformed by economic activity?

Solow's answer: 'Certainly, and I welcome any attempts to model the dependence in a transparent way, so that it can be incorporated into aggregative economics.'

Comment: One should take Solow at his word about what he now welcomes. His recent concern about the greenhouse effect is certainly welcomed by ecological economists.

However, if one agrees that the macroeconomy is a subsystem embedded in an ecosystem that is finite, non-growing, and materially closed, then wouldn't one expect the macroeconomy to have an optimal scale relative to the total ecosystem – a scale beyond which its growth is uneconomic? Why is it that each micro activity has an optimal scale, while the aggregate of all microeconomic activities is supposed to grow for ever, unconstrained by any notion of optimal scale of the macroeconomy relative to the ecosystem? Ecological economists would welcome any attempts by Solow to model the limit to growth resulting from optimal scale of the macroeconomy.

5. Do you believe that the matter/energy transformations required by economic activity are constrained by the entropy law?

Solow's answer: 'No doubt everything is subject to the entropy law, but this is of no immediate practical importance for modeling what is after all a brief instant of time in a small corner of the universe.'

Comment: Solow seems to identify the entropy law only with the ultimate heat death of the universe. I don't worry much about that either, and neither did Georgescu-Roegen, whose critique of Solow was not based on such a remote cosmic event. But the entropy law has more immediate and relevant implications: that you can't burn the same lump of coal twice; that when you do burn it once you get soot, ashes, CO_2 and waste heat, as well as useful heat. The entropy law also tells us that recycling energy is always a losing proposition, that there are limits to the efficiency of conversion of energy from one form to another, and that there is a practical limit to materials recycling – all in the here and now, not just in the cosmic by and by. Would Solow suggest to engineers designing real production recipes that they can neglect the second law of thermodynamics because we are concerned only with 'a brief instant of time in a small corner of the universe'?

Low-entropy matter/energy is the physical coordinate of usefulness, the basic necessity that humans must use up but cannot create, and for which the human economy is totally dependent on nature's services. Entropy is the qualitative difference that distinguishes useful resources from an equal quantity of useless waste. Solow's statement that entropy is 'of no immediate practical importance' to economic life is evidence in support of Georgescu-Roegen's indictment that Solow 'must have a very erroneous view of the economic process as a whole'. In any event Georgescu-Roegen's criticisms remain unanswered.

10 A note on neoclassical production theory and alchemy

Output (Y) is measured as a flow in neoclassical production functions, while capital (K) and labour (L) are measured as stocks, or more correctly as the service of the stock during the same time period over which the output flow is measured. In the usual representation, $Y = f(K, L)$, we have a flow of material output generated by two stock inputs which are continually available, but are not decumulated, during the time period over which Y is measured. Is it possible for stocks, by themselves, to yield a flow? An economist's first reaction is to say of course a stock by itself can yield a flow – consider the stock of money in the bank yielding by itself a flow of interest (the principal is not decumulated yet the interest flow continues, perhaps even in perpetuity). True, but that is a convention of finance, not a physical process of production. OK, how about a stock of cattle yielding a flow of new cattle in a sustained-yield fashion – is that not a physical stock yielding a physical flow? Not really – it is a stock (livestock) converting a *flow* of inputs (grass, grain) into a *flow* of outputs (new cattle, and waste products). The resource inflow of grass and grains, and so on is *transformed* into a product outflow of new cattle (and replacement to the livestock herd for natural mortality or 'depreciation'), plus waste. The correct description of 'production' is transformation of a resource inflow into product outflows, with stocks of capital and labour functioning as the transforming agents. This is not only true for the living transformers in agriculture (plants and animals), but even more obviously true for industrial processes of production where the transformation is visible within the factory at every stage.

Economists cannot be ignorant of such basic facts. Why then do they choose to ignore them, to exclude natural resources from theoretical analysis right from the start? Perhaps it is a case of 'money fetishism' – assuming that what is true for money in the bank, the symbol and measure of wealth, 'must' be true for the wealth that it symbolizes. Some support for this hypothesis comes from Michael Common's observations on the treatment of resources in a typical, well-respected microeconomics textbook (Varian, 1987). The minimal attention paid to natural resources consists in deriving the Hotelling rule, noting that 'the argument boils down to this simple idea: oil in the ground is like money in the bank'. The next section of Varian's textbook considers when to cut a forest, and as Common notes, 'it turns out that the argument here also boils down to the simple idea that a forest is like money in the bank' (Common, 1997). This would seem to be a case of what A.N. Whitehead called the 'fallacy of misplaced concreteness' – that is, identifying one abstracted conceptual aspect with the total concrete reality from which it has been abstracted.

Alternatively, perhaps the absense of material flows reflects an anthropocentric unwillingness on the part of neoclassical economists (unlike the physiocrats, and even the classical economists) to concede to nature any role in the creation of value, and consequently any claim to a share of the total product. Acceptance of the dogma that nature makes no contribution to production allows some neoclassical economists to assume that any increase in production not explained by increases in labour or capital must be the result of some other humanly created factor, namely technology. Such economists do not flinch from claiming that the 50 per cent unexplained residual, usually found when they attempt to fit $Y = f(K,L)$ to historical data, must really be a measure of technological progress (human ingenuity). In fact the residual is a measure of the effect on Y of everything that is not labour and capital, including, of course, natural resources. To make matters worse, as Georgescu-Roegen pointed out, capital and labour themselves require a material inflow for their own production, replacement and maintenance.

The function $Y = f(K,L)$ is a gross misrepresentation of production. Even in the rare instances when natural resource inputs (R) are included along with K and L, it is done in such a way (using Cobb–Douglas or other multiplicative functions) that, mathematically, K can substitute for R, as R approaches zero, without limiting the size of Y. No one doubts the mathematics *per se* – just whether the particular mathematical representation reflects the essence of the real world process of production. One cannot but seriously doubt that we can produce a thousand-pound cake with just a few ounces of flour, sugar, and so on, if only we stir harder with bigger spoons and use a bigger oven!

My (Georgescu-Roegen's) argument has to do only with substitution of K for R. No one questions the possibilities of substitution between L and K, or among different natural recources. There are, however, good empirical reasons for believing that substitution between K and R is very marginal and that the dominant relation is one of complementarity. It is a *fact* that R is the inflow being transformed into an outflow by the agency of capital and labour. It is a *fact* that transforming agent (efficient cause) and material being transformed (material cause) require each other. It is a *fact* that substitution possibilities are confined to a very small margin – that margin determined by possibilities of cutting waste of materials in process down to zero. The *fact* that capital also requires resources in its own production is a further element of complementarity when one takes the aggregate view, as these macro production functions do. It is also an *empirical fact* that Y cannot embody more materials or energy than were present in R, and that there is an entropic degradation required by the transformation – that is, the entropy of the product output flow plus the waste output flow is higher than the entropy of the resource input flow. In a finite, 'full' world in which natural sources of low-entropy matter/energy and natural sinks for high-entropy matter/energy are both scarce, economists can continue to theorize on the basis of the neoclassical production function only at great peril to themselves and everyone else. Such theorizing is worse than irrelevant – it is actively misleading.

One may claim that my argument is merely theoretical rather than empirical. But the 'theories' I appeal to are *factually* the best-grounded ones we have (they are usually considered 'laws'). By contrast econometric measurements focus mainly on the elasticity of substitution of K for L, which, for our discussion, (a) is not the relevant substitution; and (b) consists of widely varying estimates of a physical misrepresentation, that is, they begin with a factually erroneous relationship, and then proceed to measure it inaccurately. A necessary category, R, is totally missing in such empirical investigations – a recipe with no ingredients.[1] The elasticity of substitution of stirring for baking is rather meaningless if there is nothing either to stir or bake.

Either production is a process of transformation of a resource inflow (material cause) into product outflows, using labour and capital as agents of transformation (efficient cause), all transformations subject to the laws of thermodynamics, or else it is an alchemical alembic in which reactions are supposed to be governed by hermetic manipulation (multiplication in this case) of occult symbols. The neoclassical production function is worse than alchemy – the alchemists at least respected the law of conservation of mass, even though they failed to recognize all the restrictions to which transmutations of that constant mass are subject. Neoclassical economists, without blushing, write equations in which material output flows require no material input flows. Financial conventions of money in the bank earning interest – a stock by itself yielding a flow – have become the lens through which economists view the physical process of production. This is such a fundamental error that few people are able to believe that economists could have made it, much less persist in it. Consequently most people acquiesce in the error, believing that those who point it out must be mistaken. This is a reasonable enough attitude until one has had time to think and to search out the suspected mistake. The critique here outlined was in its essence made 25 years ago by Georgescu-Roegen. How much time should one search in vain for a mistake, before deciding that there is no mistake? Has anyone even been searching?

Before attempting a better analytical representation of the process of production than that of the neoclassical production function, we should be clear why the latter fails. By excessive abstraction it throws away important and solid information. It tells us merely that output is a function of inputs. But *how* do the inputs combine to produce the output? Perhaps due to an exessively literal interpretation of the words 'factor' and 'product', economists have assumed that the obvious manner of transformation of factors into product is by multiplication! In the usual Cobb–Douglas specifications, K, L and R are multiplied by each other – and multiplied by themselves, each being raised to an exponent. Economists have been so bemused by the mathematical convenience of such functions that they have overlooked a serious defect – namely, there is no multiplication going on in the real world. It is not the case that $2K$ times $3L$ times $4R$ gives us $24KLR$ equal to $24Y$. If such were the case there would be enormous possibilities for substitution among all three factors, not to mention the alchemical creation of matter *ex nihilo*. As argued above, the relation of resource flows to capital or labour funds is overwhelmingly one of complementarity, even though there may be considerable substitution between funds (K and L), or among the various particular resources composing R.

The only thing embodied in the product is R. As Georgescu-Roegen noted, the only thing we want to find in our new coat is the cloth and thread, nicely combined – if we were to find in our coat the tailor's needle, or a piece of his finger, we should surely consider that very regrettable! The key feature of production, abstracted from in the neoclassical production function, is that the resource inflow is transformed into a product outflow by the agency of capital and labour funds. The physical process is one of transformation of resources, not multiplication of 'factors'.

Figure 10.1 gives us a starting point for a more accurate analytical description of production as transformation. In the diagram resource inflows are transformed into outflows of products and wastes. The products are also ultimately transformed into waste by use. The waste flow returns to nature as pollution where it is absorbed, and ultimately reconstituted into usable resources by the agency of biogeochemical cycles powered by the sun. These 'new' resources are again depleted (extracted), and again transformed into products by the agency of funds of capital and labour. Funds of labour and capital are themselves physical structures that require maintenance and replacement out of the product flow, if the process is to keep going in the face of wear and tear, death and depreciation. Ultimately, over the long run, the whole system runs on solar energy, but were it not for the terrestrial material structures capable of capturing that solar energy (natural capital), the earth would be a barren planet, bathed in abundant sunshine, but, like the moon, incapable of supporting life and wealth.

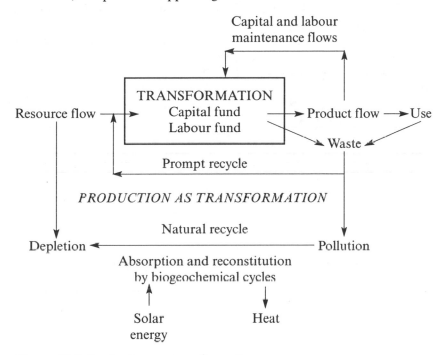

Figure 10.1 Production as transformation

Incomplete though it remains, is not Figure 10.1 a far more revealing representation of production than the insipid $Y = K^a L^b R^c$? Is it not clear that 'production' is really the transformation of the inflow R into the outflow Y by the agency of the funds of K and L? The size of the K and L funds determines the rate at which the resource inputs can be transformed into product outputs (and waste). Of course the size of each of the funds is positively correlated with the product obtained by multiplying the two funds together, so statistically one might model the rate of transformation as dependent on the product of K and L, although there is no theory of transformation that suggests that anything like multiplication is going on in the real world. The multiplicative description once again would build in the assumption of substitutability rather than complementarity, this time between K and L. There are better reasons for assuming substitution between K and L than between K and R, but still the specific process of transformation often imposes complementarity between K and L. Why prejudge the issue with a multiplicative form? Indeed, even addition of K and L would reflect an assumption of substitutability. Assuming complementarity of K and L, the absolute size of the smaller of the two transforming agents (limiting factor) determines the rate at which the resource inflow can be transformed into a product outflow. To give further specification in the interest of mathematical tractability and ease of statistical modelling has, as we have seen, the significant cost of introducing spurious assumptions that give rise to misleading implications. To cite William of Ockham with a bit more literalism than he intended, 'Entities should not be multiplied beyond necessity.'

Note

1. Such empiricism is reminiscent of Borges' nutty ancient Chinese classification of animals: '(1) all animals belonging to the emperor, (2) embalmed animals, (3) tame animals, (4) animals appearing no bigger than a mosquito when viewed from a far distance', and so on. Maybe I exaggerate in this comparison, but one wonders what useful purpose could be served by empirical description of either set of categories, no matter how meticulously and rigorously done.

References

Common, M. (1997), 'Is Georgescu-Roegen versus Solow/Stiglitz the Important Question?', *Ecological Economics*, **22**, September.
Varian, H.R. (1987), *Intermediate Microeconomics: A Modern Approach*, New York: Norton.

11 Thermodynamic and economic concepts as related to resource-use policies: comment*

Burness et al. (1980) state that 'the relevance of the Second Law is its restriction on the amount of work that one can obtain from any system'. While this is certainly a minimal statement, it nevertheless correctly suggests that the entropy law should be viewed as a constraint, not as an independent, sufficient explanation of value. It is somewhat surprising therefore, that, as the authors proceed to argue in favour of neoclassical business as usual and against any special role for entropy, they should do so on the grounds that entropy does not provide an alternative, independent explanation of value. The role of entropy as a constraint is not mentioned again. Proponents of the view that entropy is relevant are invited to answer a number of questions concerning the mechanism by which energy (or entropy) is supposed to determine prices.

This invitation to answer specific questions is certainly a fair and reasonable procedure on the authors' part, and I will respond to it in a minute. But first it must be pointed out that the authors are looking for relevance in the wrong place. In fairness it must be admitted that some ecologists (Odom, 1971; Costanza, 1981) have proposed just such an energy-based substitute for market valuation as the authors attack, and I share their scepticism regarding this claim, even while valuing the work of these ecologists for other reasons. But to include Georgescu-Roegen in this school, as the authors do, is quite wrong and leads to much confusion. For an explicit disproof of the energy theory of value, see Georgescu-Roegen (1981, esp. pp. 68–70).

Burness et al. state that 'Georgescu-Roegen claims an entropy theory of value; . . . however, the authors find his arguments in this regard to be inscrutable.' The reason they find his arguments 'inscrutable' is that he is not arguing for an entropy theory of value. On the contrary, he specifically cautions against such an interpretation. Moreover, Burness et al. themselves, in another context (their fn. 9), quote Georgescu-Roegen on the reasons why an entropy theory of value would be unsatisfactory! I emphasize their misreading of Georgescu-Roegen because, first, it underlies their misconception of how the entropy law

* Published in *Land Economics*, **62** (3), August 1986, pp. 319–22.

is relevant to economics, and second, because Georgescu-Roegen (1971) is both the leading proponent of the entropy view and the only economist of that persuasion cited by our four authors. Thus, if they misread Georgescu-Roegen then they have misunderstood the issue they are addressing. It is a big mistake to think that his arguments are at all affected by demolishing someone else's 'energy theory of value'.

With this preliminary out of the way we can now turn to the main purpose of this note, which is to respond to the specific questions raised by the authors. Each of the four questions will be quoted, followed by a reply.

(1) 'Is the relevant system of values to be one wherein individual preferences determine values? If not, what is the mechanism that determines value? For example, are values somehow dictated on the basis of "work" in particular, or energy in general?'

There is no substitution of market values by calculated, non-market coefficients based on work or energy or entropy. It has long been known, though recently downplayed, that not all values are expressible through individual preferences interacting under individual constraints to determine prices in a competitive market. In the light of the entropy law a previously neglected aggregate constraint on the physical scale of the economy relative to the ecosystem is seen to exist. The market is, by itself, unable to reflect this constraint because Pareto optimality of allocation is independent of whether or not the scale of physical throughput is ecologically sustainable (Pearce, 1976). It is worth taking account of this aggregate constraint on scale only if we collectively value sustainability, a value which, like that of justice, is not expressible at the level of individual choices in a competitive market. For the value of sustainability and the constraint on aggregate physical scale to be reflected in market prices, there must be a collectively enacted constraint on the aggregate flow (throughput) of matter and energy from the ecosystem through the economy, and back to the ecosystem. This constraint must be set, not according to prices, but according to criteria of sustainability. Operating under this newly instituted biophysical constraint, the market will, at the micro level, come up with a different set of prices which now reflect the social value of sustainability, which, thanks to the newly recognized biophysical constraint, is no longer implicitly treated as a free good.

The nature of the economic constraint imposed by the laws of thermodynamics is two-fold. The first law tells us that matter and energy inputs are not created *ex nihilo*, but must be extracted from the environment, and that outputs must return to the environment in various forms which add up to equal the quantity of inputs. The second law says that although total input equals total output in quantitative terms, there is a big qualitative difference between the equal quantities of raw material inputs and ultimate waste outputs. Raw material is low-entropy matter–energy, waste is high-entropy matter–energy. Furthermore, both low-entropy sources and high-entropy sinks are finite in a finite environment, and the sinks cannot be recycled into sources on human time scales. Finitude would not be so restrictive were it not for entropy, for then finite matter and energy could be recycled ever faster. Nor would the entropy law be so confining were it not for finitude, since infinite sources and sinks would obviate any need for recycling. But if both finitude and entropy are real (as indeed they are), then the physical scale of the economy and its supporting throughput cannot increase indefinitely. To put it in a nutshell, if the qualitative difference between equal quantities of raw material and waste material is not relevant to economics, then what is? Entropy is the measure of that qualitative difference.

The market is sensitive to scale issues at the micro level, but is insensitive to the macro-level scale of the whole economy relative to the ecosystem. The fact that the market can substitute relatively abundant resources for relatively scarce ones is a great virtue, but does not remove the entropic constraint. Substitutability among various types of low entropy does not mean that there can be a substitute for low entropy itself.

(2) 'Can one define in some precise way those dimensions of the First and Second Laws which are reflected in markets? If so, what is the rationale for arguing that they should be reflected?'

The previous reply dealt with this question in part, but a few more comments seem warranted.

What is not reflected in the market is the value of the optimal sustainable physical scale of the economy relative to the ecosystem. The market does not distinguish an ecologically sustainable scale of matter–energy throughput from an unsustainable scale, just as it does not distinguish between ethically just and unjust distributions of income. Sustainability, like justice, is a value not achievable by purely individualistic market processes. Yet these values can be reflected back into market prices when the market operates under collectively instituted macro constraints designed to protect these values to which the purely individualistic market is blind.

A distinction should be made between 'price-determined' and 'price-determining' decisions. The criteria underlying the collective setting of the aggregate constraints are ecological and ethical. These ecological and ethical decisions are price-determining, not price-determined. The allocation of the ecologically sustainable aggregate throughput among millions of alternative uses at the micro level is price-determined – that is, determined by the corrected prices reflecting the newly recognized collective constraint. The entropy law helps us to understand the nature and necessity of this constraint on scale and growth. But it offers no alternative principle of evaluation that substitutes for markets.

(3) 'If one can argue for an "energy value" that is somehow distinct from market values, what are the manifestations or signals of (from) this value? How is the energy price, or other value measure, determined and used in the process of resource allocation and policy formulation?'

Since question (3) is predicated on contrary answers to questions (1) and (2), I will not comment specifically on it.

(4) 'Acknowledging market imperfections, equity issues, and market distortions related to government policies, what is the mechanism by which recognition of thermodynamic laws is to resolve, or marginally contribute to resolving, these problems? Policy ramifications based on economic concepts would generally lead to adjustments in price mechanisms (for example, subsidies, taxes, decontrol) to adjust for externalities and distortions in scarcity values: What is the energy counterpart to these market-related mechanisms?'

As already indicated in previous replies, there is no 'energy counterpart to market-related mechanisms' in correcting for the market's failure to respect the constraint on scale and the value of sustainability. Several market-related policies have been suggested for institutionalizing such a constraint, including a depletion quota auction (Daly, 1980), a national *ad valorem* severance tax (Page, 1980), and an energy tax-cum-rebate scheme (Hannon, 1980).

There is no need to discuss these alternative policy suggestions here because the point at issue is whether the entropy law is relevant to economics, not what is the best policy for dealing with entropic constraints once we have recognized their relevance. There is, however, one very prevalent misunderstanding that should be guarded against, namely the idea that entropy and sustainability are 'only' ethical issues and that the whole question simply boils down to a claim that society's values are wrong. On the contrary, entropy is a physical law, like gravity, and entropic constraints (depletion and pollution) are objective facts evident in the present, not value judgements, and not speculation about future millennia. How we react to this objective condition, whether by emphasizing sustainability or temporary extravagance as the dominant goal, is certainly a value judgement. One may reject sustainability ('après moi le déluge'), but that does not abolish the entropy law. It just means that one has made a value judgement in favour of temporary extravagance. 'Furthermore, suppose that society did value sustainability as a social goal (who can rule that out?). Could the market by itself reflect that goal in relative prices, or does it need an institutional recognition of the entropic constraint? I have argued above that the latter is the case, that sustainability, like justice, is a public good not attainable by individualistic market processes alone. We may disagree on how important sustainability should be as a social goal, but that hardly makes entropy into an ethical issue.

Why is the entropy law still so 'unpopular' with neoclassical economists? In part because they mistakenly associate it with an 'energy theory of value'. But also perhaps the answer has something to do with the negative implications of the entropy law for any ideology based on continuous growth.

References

Burness, Stuart, Ronald Cummings, Glen Morris and Inja Paik (1980), 'Thermodynamic and Economic Concepts as Related to Resource-Use Policies', *Land Economics* **56** (Feb.), pp. 1–9.

Costanza, Robert (1981), 'Embodied Energy, Energy Analysis, and Economics', in *Energy, Economics, and the Environment*, H.E. Daly (ed.), Boulder, CO. Westview Press.

Daly, H.E. (1980), 'The Steady State Economy,' in H.E. Daly (ed.), *Economics, Ecology, Ethics*, San Francisco: W.H. Freeman and Co.

Georgescu-Roegen, Nicholas (1971), *The Entropy Law and the Economic Process*, Cambridge, MA: Harvard University Press.

Georgescu-Roegen, Nicholas (1981), 'Energy, Matter, and Economic Valuation: Where Do We Stand?' in H.E. Daly (ed.), *Energy Economics, and the Environment*, Boulder, CO: Westview Press.

Hannon, Bruce (1980), 'Energy Use and Moral Restraint', in H.E. Daly (ed.), *Economics, Ecology, Ethics*, San Francisco: W.H. Freeman and Co.

Odum, Howard (1971), *Environment, Power, and Society*, New York. Wiley Interscience.

Page, Talbot (1980), 'The Severance Tax as an Instrument of Intertemporal Equity.' in H.E. Daly (ed.), *Economics, Ecology, Ethics*, San Francisco: W.H. Freeman Co.

Pearce, David W. (1976), *Environmental Economics*, London: Longman. See especially ch. 4.

12 Comment: Is the entropy law relevant to the economics of natural resource scarcity? – Yes, of course it is!*

Several points in Jeffrey T. Young's paper (Young, 1991), which gives a negative answer to the question in the title, require comment. The first part of the article does not elicit any quarrel from me in so far as it describes the view that I hold, namely that entropy is fundamental to economics. This view stems mainly from the work of Georgescu-Roegen. The only thing that I object to in this first part is the statement that 'the entropy law is being recommended to us as the basis of a new energy and/or entropy theory of value'. This is a totally incorrect statement taken from Burness et al. (1980). I took pains to correct their error in a comment in the same journal (Daly, 1986), and I would have appreciated it if Young had paid attention to that correction and avoided repetition of the error. For the rest, however, Young's model is, as he claims, 'faithful to their conception of the economic process'. It is significant that there is nothing in Young's model of the 'entropy view' that implies or requires an energy or entropy theory of value, which makes the extraneous introduction of this error difficult to understand.

Young's fundamental criticism is that entropy is 'an anthropomorphic concept intimately associated with what is useful and, therefore, defined by current technology'. The fact that entropy has an anthropomorphic aspect relating to usefulness in no way implies that it is defined by current technology. Also, Young thinks that the material interpretation is critical to the relevance of entropy to economics and that his criticism applies only to entropy as material dispersion. But in fact his arguments extend to energy as well. The obvious anthropomorphism of usefulness and also the relation to technology both apply to entropy in strict energy terms as well as in its looser material interpretation. The problem for Young is that recognition of the general nature of his criticism would involve him in proving far too much – namely that the entropy law is false in its classical formulation for energy! Yet he never explains why his arguments do not apply to energy as well as to matter.

Physicists routinely apply entropy to matter, and, although this exten-

* Published in *Journal of Environmental Economics and Management*, **23**, July 1992, pp. 91–5. The views expressed in this article are those of the author and should in no way be attributed to the World Bank.

sion may involve some difficulties, it is far more than a mere analogy. Our inability to reduce different forms of matter to a common denominator in the way we can do for energy prevents us from determining whether we will eventually use up more matter in the recycling effort than the amount recycled. But it remains clear that complete materials recycling would require ruinous amounts of energy and time.

To demonstrate his objection Young asks us to consider a world with two material resources: a known resource *a* and a newly recognized resource *b*. As *a* is depleted from concentrated mineral deposits and used, it eventually becomes dispersed in the environment. The material stock has become less orderly, more entropic. But suppose now the discovery that another mineral, *b*, is also useful, thanks to a new technology. Then if we add ordered deposits of *b* to the picture it might more than make up for the increased disorder or randomness in *a*, and thus entropy would have declined rather than increased as a result of new knowledge, which is anti-entropic according to Young. Why exactly the same observations would not apply to old and new energy sources is not explained. After all, energy does not disappear any more than matter does – it too is dispersed, and new discoveries of concentrated energy might more than offset energy degradation caused by economic activity in a given year.

This argument is strange in several other ways. New knowledge will naturally change any system in which it is discovered, regardless of whether that system incorporates the entropy law or the 'canonical neoclassical assumptions'. If we discover a novel resource, *b*, or even if we just discover more deposits of the same resource, *a*, the result is the same – namely, we must redescribe the state of the system, taking account of the new knowledge. That new description, based on new knowledge, would record a stock of low-entropy materials greater (and likewise in the case of energy) than that in the previous inventory. This does not mean that the economic process is not entropic or even that knowledge is anti-entropic – it only means that our description of the initial stock of low-entropy materials was incomplete in the light of new knowledge. Perhaps the upward bookkeeping revision of inventory of low-entropy materials might be greater in a given year than the physical increase in entropy from resource extraction and use. That hardly reverses the entropic direction of economic activity. It may be claimed that new knowledge will expand available matter (and energy) faster than economic activity will convert it into unavailable matter (and energy). This could happen, but so could the reverse. New knowledge may reduce available matter–energy. For example, the greenhouse effect represents new knowledge that lowers the effective availability of fossil fuels because the capacity to absorb the dispersed CO_2 is less than previously thought. New knowledge may reveal new limits. The hole in the ozone layer is new knowledge. To suppose, as is usually done, that new knowledge will always expand the resource base and never contract it is to overspecify the content of new knowledge, which must always be something of a surprise – and not necessarily a pleasant one.

Georgescu-Roegen (1981) claims to have discovered a fourth law of thermodynamics to the effect that matter will dissipate in a closed system (that is, a system closed with respect to matter but with a plentiful throughput of energy), or, alternatively, that complete recycling is impossible. I am prepared to believe in common-sense evidence that for all practical purposes complete recycling is impossible, but I am not competent to assess the claim that it is physically impossible, so I leave that to the physicists. But for present purposes it does not matter whether Georgescu-Roegen is right or wrong about his fourth law.

What matters is a *non sequitur* in Young's fundamental argument:

> Is *b* available matter when there are no known uses for it? If so, then how can we know that dissipated *a* is unavailable? The absence of a technology for using dissipated *a* would not mean it is unavailable matter. The point is that available matter is dependent on the existence of appropriate technologies. It is not a purely physical concept.

If new knowledge can lead to a new use for low-entropy material resource, *b*, then why can it not find a technology for using dissipated old resource *a*? But a new use for a new source of low entropy tells us nothing at all about the possibility of finding a new use for the dissipated high-entropy remains of old resources. In both cases Young thinks we are doing the same thing – simply converting non-available into available matter through technology. To call both dissipated *a* and concentrated *b* (before discovery) by the same name, 'unavailable matter', and then reason that, if technology can turn previously 'unavailable' *b* into a useful resource, then surely it can do the same for newly unavailable *a*, is a gross *non sequitur*. The reasons for the unavailability of *a* and *b* are entirely different – *a* is unavailable because it is physically dispersed, and *b* is unavailable because, although concentrated, we have as yet no knowledge of how to use it.

Does the fact that we discovered uses for aluminium imply that we can invent a technology to recycle all the particles of rubber scraped from tyres on kerbs and interstate highways? The difference is that there is a technology for using aluminium that is economic, but the known technologies for recycling rubber particles on highways are not economic. The main reason for that fact is that aluminium deposits are concentrated, and scraped rubber particles are highly dispersed. One recycling technology for rubber particles requires many people on their hands and knees using magnifying glasses and tweezers. That is not likely to be economic. Whether it is inevitable that more matter will be dissipated in the form of worn-out tweezers and skinned knees than will be recycled in the form of gathered rubber particles is a nice question that I cannot answer. However, it is clear to me that tweezer-based recycling of specks of rubber (or vacuum cleaning or sand blasting technology) will be ruinously expensive in terms of energy, labour and time regardless of the exact balance of materials dissipation. Since disordered matter requires more energy for processing, and since that extra energy will at some point make the recycling of dispersed matter uneconomic, we need no rigorous law of material entropy with a physical (as opposed to an economic) limit on recycling matter. This economic limit stems from the physical fact that enormous amounts of energy, as well as of other materials, are required to recycle highly dispersed matter.

Even in the case of energy it is not that it is physically impossible to recycle degraded energy, but rather that it always costs more energy to carry out the recycling than the amount recycled. So recycling energy is always *uneconomic* (regardless of the price of energy!). This economic aspect of the entropy law (not only admitted but *emphasized* by Georgescu-Roegen as the main reason that economists need to pay attention to entropy) does *not* mean that entropy is subject to technology. Technology remains subject to entropy. Perpetual motion technologies remain undiscovered. If it were really so easy for technology to turn available matter (dispersed a) back into available matter (concentrated a), then why is someone not filtering sea water for molecules of gold and petroleum? And if recycling dispersed matter were as easy as finding new resources, then why have even neoclassical economists put the emphasis on substitution of new resources rather than on recycling of old resources, that is on finding b rather than recycling a?

It is possible to invent technologies that are able economically to exploit lower concentrations of minerals than were exploited previously. The tailings of old silver mines are used as ore for new processes. But the new process too ends up with tailings that it cannot reuse. New technology can more efficiently extract usefulness from the entropic degradation of the matter–energy throughout, but it cannot thereby become anti-entropic. Tailings that can be mined again are like water that has flowed part of the way to the sea, but still has a way to go. Mining tailings are not like having water run uphill.

Young states that 'the model of entropic decay is not relevant for modeling open systems'. This seems quite wrong to me. An organism is an open system that maintains itself in a kind of steady state that is far from thermodynamic equilibrium (death and decay). It does this by counteracting its tendency to entropic decay by 'sucking low entropy from its environment', as Schroedinger (1945) put it. The basic physical understanding of life is that it is an open system that imports low entropy from the environment and exports high entropy back to the environment, thereby maintaining its highly ordered structure in a quasi-steady state. It is one thing to recognize that open systems can *resist* entropic decay and something else to claim that entropic decay is *not relevant* to open systems.

Economies, like organisms, consist of ordered structures subject to entropic decay, but capable of building up their internal order at the expense of imposing greater disorder on their environment. Economies resist entropic decay by importing low-entropy matter–energy from the environment and exporting high-entropy matter–energy back to the environment. This throughput or metabolic flow is necessarily entropic in both cases. At the input end it takes low-entropy matter–energy from finite environment sources, and at the output end it returns high-entropy wastes to finite environmental sinks. The sources become depleted, and the sinks fill up and become polluted. The entropy law is supremely relevant because it says that sinks cannot serve as sources. Absolute scarcity arises from the *combination* of the first and second laws of thermodynamics, not from either alone. If sources and sinks were infinite (or could be created and destroyed) then it would not matter that the flow between them was entropic and irreversible; if sources and sinks were finite but no entropy law existed, then we could turn sinks into sources, recycle everything, and burn the same gallon of gas over and over. In the light of such basic facts it is difficult to understand how anyone could claim that the entropy law is not relevant to resource scarcity. Even if one considers the sun to be an infinite source and space to be an infinite sink, it is only the total stock of solar energy that is quasi-infinite – its flow rate of arrival to earth is strictly limited. Nor would it be intelligent to increase it by 'mining' the sun even if we could, because increasing the rate of insolation would be ecologically very disruptive.

We should not appeal to thermodynamics for temporally parochial measures of exchange value or relative scarcity, that is, prices that measure scarcity relative to wants in the service of optimally allocating a given resource flow among alternative human uses in the present generation. But the question of absolute scarcity, of the optimal sustainable scale of the economic subsystem as a part of the overall ecosystem, cannot be understood without some help from thermodynamics (Daly, 1991).

With regard to the charge of 'scientism' levelled at those who recognize and insist on the relevance of the entropy law to resource scarcity, I would like to plead innocent and to reverse the charge. It is not scientism to respect the effect of basic physical laws like gravity, entropy and conservation of mass on economic activity. It is scientism to believe that applied science through technology can reverse these basic physical laws. The entropy law has implications that are unfriendly to the regnant ideology of growth as the economic *sumum bonum*. There is a strong tendency to resist such implications. But there is hope that they will not be resisted for ever. The law of conservation of mass is now generally respected among economists, even though it has implications unfriendly to the growth ideology. Nevertheless, conservation of mass is still implicitly denied by devotees of the unlimited substitution of capital for resources in Cobb–Douglas production functions. Young, however, shows signs of independence from the growth ideology by forthrightly pointing out that recognition of the first law of thermodynamics 'may constrain our optimism with regard to the sustainability of economic growth'. If he continues to think about it, I would bet that he comes to see that the entropy law greatly increases the force of this constraint.

References

Burness, S., R. Cummings, G. Morris and I. Paik (1980), 'Thermodynamic and economic concepts as related to resource-use policies', *Land Economics*, **56** (Feb.), pp. 1–9.

Daly, H.E. (1986), 'Thermodynamic and economic concepts as related to resource-use policies: Comment', *Land Economics*, **63** (3), pp. 319–22.

Daly, H.E. (1991), 'Towards an environmental macroeconomics', *Land Economics*, **67** (2), pp. 255–9.

Georgescu-Roegen, N. (1981), 'Energy, matter, and economic valuation: Where do we stand?', in H.E. Daly and A.F. Umaña (eds), *Energy, Economics, and the Environment*, Boulder, CO: Westview Press.

Schroedinger, E. (1945), *What is Life?*, New York: Macmillan.

Young, J.T. (1991), 'Is the entropy law relevant to the economics of natural resource scarcity?', *Journal of Environmental Economics and Management*, **21**, pp. 167–79.

IV On economic development and population

Introduction

'We make the world by the questions we ask', said physicist John Wheeler. If we ask only neoclassical questions we make a neoclassical world. If we ask neo-Malthusian questions we make a neo-Malthusian world. Chapter 13 illustrates this in reviewing the report of the Working Group on Population Growth and Economic Development by the prestigious National Academy of Sciences Committee on Population. The report was more notable for the question not asked than for the questions it did consider.

Chicago School economist and Nobel Laureate Gary Becker, with Nigel Tomes, developed a model of intergenerational distribution of wealth and income, based on individualistic utility maximization. To make the mathematics work they were forced to assume that people reproduced asexually. I thought this was going too far in the direction of 'saving the model from the real world', and wrote the critique included here as Chapter 14. I submitted it as a comment to the *Journal of Political Economy* which had published the Becker and Tomes article. They sent it to Becker for comment, which was appropriate. But to my surprise they sent it *only* to Becker, who advised against publication, alleging that the assumption of asexual reproduction was for analytical convenience only and not logically necessary for the model, a claim with which I disagreed, but with which the editor, Becker's University of Chicago colleague, concurred. I suggested that the opinion of a more neutral third party be solicited. That suggestion was rejected. Consequently I published the comment in another journal. So much for open debate and discussion in prestigious academic journals! I think my comment is important because it shows both how extremely individualistic neoclassical economists are, and how just a little pressure at a critical point can bring a complicated neoclassical model tumbling down. Of course, Becker and Tomes may claim that with the advent of cloning asexual reproduction has become a reality and their extreme individualism is vindicated. Maybe so, but I believe that cloning requires an egg, so only women could truly clone themselves in a strictly asexual manner. More importantly, one's clone is no more the same individual person as one's self than one's identical twin would be.

13 Population Growth and Economic Development: Policy Questions* – a review

This little book has an excellent format. It asks nine specific questions and offers four or five pages of discussion and answer for each one. Most questions are of the form: Will slower population growth ... do this or that? Will it increase per capita income through greater per capita availability of exhaustible resources? Of renewable resources? Will it alleviate pollution and environmental degradation? Will it increase worker productivity? Levels of schooling and health? Absorption into the modern sector? Will it reduce technological innovation and economies of scale by lowering density? And finally, does a couple's fertility behaviour impose costs on society at large? Since this review will be mainly critical of the report, I want to say at the outset that it contains much of value. The questions asked are relevant; the answers are informative, readable and brief. How then is it possible to be critical of such a report? What more could one want? Quite a lot, it will be seen. As physicist John Wheeler says, 'We make the world by the questions we ask.' There are other questions that make other worlds.

The main problem with the book is that it is written wholly within the intellectual discipline (mental straitjacket) of neoclassical economics. Like other neoclassical writings on population/resources/environment, this book suffers from a total failure to distinguish the problem of optimal allocation of resources from the problem of optimal scale of the entire economy relative to the ecosystem in which the economy is physically embedded as a fully dependent subsystem. In this review I would like to ask the authors (the Working Group on Population Growth and Economic Development of the NAS Committee on Population) to consider with me a tenth question: 'Accepting that competitive markets allocate resources efficiently, is there any reason to believe that the market is also capable of finding the optimal scale of the economy (where scale is understood as the product of population times per capita resource use)?' The answer to this question, I will

* National Research Council, Working Group on Population Growth and Economic Development, Committee on Population. Washington, DC: National Academy Press, 1986. Review published in *Population and Development Review*, **12** (3), September 1986, pp. 582–5.

argue, is a clear no. Furthermore, the world created by this question is more classical and Malthusian than neoclassical.

The market can, at best, lead to a Pareto-optimal allocation of resources. And it can do this independently of scale. Double population size (or per capita resource use), or cut it in half, and the market still grinds out an efficient set of relative prices and a (different) Pareto optimum. There is a different Pareto optimum for each possible scale of the economy, just as there is for each possible distribution of income. The latter proposition is well known; the former is less frequently mentioned but equally true. Distribution involves an ethical question of justice. Scale involves an ecological question of sustainability. Neither is reducible to a problem of efficient allocation.

One would expect that a report on population growth and economic development would deal first and foremost with the issue of optimal scale, since population is a major determinant of scale. But instead the issue of optimal scale is not even recognized. The discussion proceeds entirely in terms of optimal allocation. Scale effects are conflated with the allocation issue by treating them as resulting from the common-property mode of market failure. Thus air or water pollution is seen as having nothing to do with the scale of population or production, and everything to do with lack of property rights in air or water. But let us assume, however unrealistically, that property rights in air have been vested in certain people, and that we have perfect internalization of the previous common-property external costs. Everyone is now paying the 'right' price for air. Then population and per capita resource use grow, and consequently the demand for air goes up. Everyone will then pay a higher price for air. The price is 'right' in both instances as far as allocation is concerned, yet the scale issue remains unsettled. If demand for air were well below carrying capacity (a concept totally absent from the book) in the first instance, then the 'right' price is zero. After demand increases due to growth in scale, let us suppose that air becomes scarce and the new 'right' price is a positive number. Given the new demand, the old zero price is no longer efficient – no argument about that. But in which situation are we better off – that in which air is a free good or that in which it has a positive price? In both instances the prices are 'right' and the neoclassical economist is happy. But one must also ask whether one scale is better than another. Maybe one scale is sustainable and the other not. Even if both are sustainable maybe we are better off with air as a free good than at a scale at which air commands a positive price. Maybe paying a higher price for air actually represents the optimum adjustment to an ever-worsening situation. As the report observes, in a different context, it is difficult to compare welfare between larger and smaller population sizes because we have to give some value to the life enjoyment of the additional people, even if everyone lives at a lower level, and we have little idea of how to do this. One pragmatic way out is to think of maximizing cumulative lives ever lived over time at some level of per capita resource use sufficient for a good life. This puts the emphasis on long-run sustainability and non-destruction of long-run carrying capacity. There is some indication that related questions may be dealt with in the commissioned, but as yet unavailable, background paper by P. Dasgupta, which I look forward to reading. However, they are not dealt with in the published report, and for the purposes of this review I have avoided the trade-off between numbers of people and per capita resource use by defining scale as the product of the two. But one point remains clear: optimal allocation tells us nothing about optimal scale.

If the environment had unlimited carrying capacity then there would be no problem of optimal scale. Since the concept of carrying capacity is not discussed, one cannot be sure just what assumptions are made regarding its limited or unlimited nature. But, as I interpret the report, the authors reject or at least downplay any notion of the 'fixity of nature' as merely a 'commonsense impression' (p. 4) that has been displaced by the more sophisticated notion that carrying capacity is continuously expandable by economic growth. In other words, economic growth makes more room for more people, without at the same time using up ecological room to accommodate the extra production implied by economic growth. Natural resources may be finite, but 'the most important resources are not natural, but artificial (plants and equipment used in production, openings in school systems, jobs, social institutions, and economic infrastructure) and so are expandable' (p. 2). Apparently limited natural resources can be substituted by 'artificial resources', which are expandable without limit, and so carrying capacity is infinitely expandable and therefore the optimum scale issue becomes unimportant in the authors' view.

But I suggest that their view is unrealistic. More plants and equipment, schools, jobs, and so on require a larger flow of resources, a larger metabolic flow from raw materials to waste. This constitutes more an additional load on carrying capacity than an enlargement of it. Technology may lighten the load of a given scale on environmental carrying capacity and thus in effect expand it, if it allows us to squeeze more welfare from a given flow of resources. But if the new technology is the kind that simply increases the resource flow per person, then it will increase the load on carrying capacity.

The authors' discussion of expandable artificial resources compen-

sating for the depletion of finite natural resources corresponds closely
to the neoclassical tenet that capital is a near perfect substitute for
resources – a notion that cannot withstand even a moment's reflection.
First of all, 'artificial resources' (capital) are themselves made from
natural resources. Second, the relation of marginal substitutability
between capital and resources is overwhelmed by the relation of average
complementarity. Neoclassical Cobb–Douglas type production functions
that allow virtually unlimited substitution of capital for resources are
clearly unrealistic. Otherwise we could make the same house with half
the lumber but two or three times as many saws!

In sum, the big failing of the report is the common neoclassical
inability or unwillingness to separate scale problems from allocation
problems, and the consequent tendency to treat issues of scale and
carrying capacity as nothing but questions of improving allocation by
better definition of property rights. Population, of all issues, is intimately
tied to scale and carrying capacity, and far too much is left out by
questions that make for us a world that is indifferent to scale, a world
in which only allocation problems exist.

The report makes hardly any mention of Chinese population policy,
which is a pity because it would illustrate the independence of allocation
and scale issues. As the Chinese are recognizing the virtues of the
market in solving the resource allocation problem, they are simultaneously rejecting *laissez-faire* market 'solutions' to the scale problem
by adopting stringent population controls. The Chinese, in policy at
least, clearly appreciate the elementary theoretical distinction between
optimal allocation and optimal scale that proved so elusive to the
Working Group.

The Preface claims that the study represents a view balanced between
the 'extreme environmentalist and extreme mercantilist' positions on
population, and finds 'little support for either the most alarmist or the
most complacent views concerning the economic effects of population
growth' (p. viii). I personally found the treatment much closer to the
complacent than to the alarmist pole, a natural consequence of ignoring
the scale issue. Furthermore, scholars who tend to be population 'boos-
ters' (Julian Simon, Herman Kahn, Ben Wattenberg) are cited
frequently and respectfully, while those nearer to the 'alarmist' end of
the spectrum (Paul Ehrlich, Garrett Hardin, Nathan Keyfitz) are not
cited at all. *The Limits to Growth* and *The Global 2000 Report* are
mentioned in passing, only to be summarily dismissed as 'pessimistic'
or 'mechanical'. I see no reason why the report should be 'balanced' or
middle-of-the-road since the truth need not lie halfway between current
extremes. If the Working Group feels that the truth is closer to Simon—

Kahn–Wattenberg than to Ehrlich–Hardin–Keyfitz, then by all means they should say so. But they should not try to have it both ways – to claim judicious and comfortable high middle ground for a position that is in fact far closer to one extreme than the other. Let me follow my own advice by flatly stating that to me Ehrlich, Hardin and Keyfitz make vastly more sense than Simon, Kahn and Wattenberg, and by confessing my astonishment that a committee of the National Academy of Sciences would make the opposite judgement. Perhaps intellectual fashion, like the hemline of dresses, oscillates between conservative mid-tibia and liberal mid-femur. Some of us who are now out of fashion are content to do as Ronald Reagan did and just wait a few years. But others have a higher degree of fashion consciousness and adaptability.

The final conclusion of the report is that while family planning programmes will not by themselves make poor countries rich, or even advance them many rungs up the ladder of development, such programmes may increase the level of welfare of couples, their children, and society as a whole to the extent that there are negative externalities in childbearing (p. 93). The Working Group certainly cannot be accused of overselling population policy of even the most voluntary kind. Nor can they be accused of having arrived at any conclusion that has not been arrived at many times before. I think a stronger conclusion is warranted, namely, that while population policy is never a sufficient condition for development, it is often a necessary condition and deserves more emphasis than it usually gets in development policy. By 'development' here I mean an improvement in the welfare of the bottom two-thirds of the population, not just an increase in average per capita gross national product. Incidentally, one of the strong points of the neoclassical vision is that it does allow some insights into the effect of population growth on income distribution, and the brief chapter on that topic whetted my appetite to read the full background report when it becomes available.

In conclusion I would like to challenge the Working Group, individually or collectively, to give their own answer to the 'tenth question' that I have discussed in this review. Of course it is too late to include it in the published report, but I am sure they will issue subsequent reports, and I urge them to devote some space to this question.

14 Chicago School individualism versus sexual reproduction: a critique of Becker and Tomes*

Gary Becker and Nigel Tomes have published 'An Equilibrium Theory of the Distribution of Income and Intergenerational Mobility'.[1] The basic framework of their model is that of individualistic utility maximiz-ation, but with the family substituted for the individual. We are told that 'the central decision makers in this essay are infinitely long-lived families with mortal members in each generation' (p. 1155), and that 'each family maximizes a utility function spanning several generations' (p. 1181). The really interesting assumption is:

> We assume that children have the same utility function as their parents and are produced without mating, or asexually. A given family then maintains its identity indefinitely, and its fortunes can be followed over as many gener-ations as desired. Asexual reproduction could be replaced without any effect on the analysis by perfect assortative mating: each person, in effect, then mates with his own image. (p. 1161)

The implications of these assumptions are then elaborated in 25 pages of algebra. Given the exceptionally heroic nature of the assumptions, one would expect a rather heroic, or at least interesting, conclusion. Nevertheless, their main conclusion is rigorously self-evident: 'We have shown that the family is more important when the degree of inherit-ability and the propensity to invest [in children] are larger' (pp. 1154 and 1182). One already knows that without making any assumptions or algebraic manipulations; how could it be otherwise? Despite this trivial result, the Becker and Tomes article is extremely interesting in that it reveals just how far some members of the Chicago School will go in amputating those limbs of human society that do not fit the Procrustean bed of individualistic utility maximization. It will be shown below that their facile substitution of family for individual as a way of extending the model to an intergenerational time frame just does not work, and that, contrary to their claim, the assumption of asexual reproduction cannot be substituted by perfect assortative mating without totally undermining the individualistic basis of the model.

* Published in *Journal of Economic Issues*, March 1982, pp. 307–12.

Let us begin with a simple proposition: One's great-great grand-children will also be the great-great grandchildren of fifteen other people in one's own generation, people whose identities cannot be determined before the fact. They could be almost any fifteen people. More generally, as is evident from the 'family tree' diagram in Figure 14.1, a given person in a given generation will normally have $2n$ ancestors in the nth previous generation.[2]

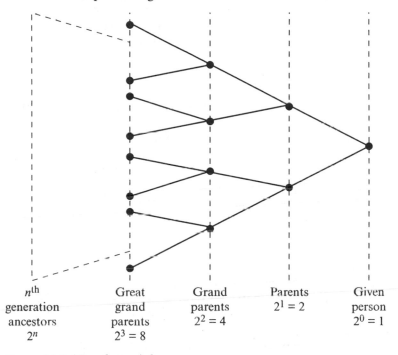

nth	Great	Grand	Parents	Given
generation	grand	parents	$2^1 = 2$	person
ancestors	parents	$2^2 = 4$		$2^0 = 1$
2^n	$2^3 = 8$			

Figure 14.1 'Family tree' diagram

Assuming that the inheritable influence (genetic and cultural, as well as monetary) exerted by the fifteen other great-great grandparents on the common descendant is as great as one's own, then it would make little sense to assume any individual responsibility for the condition of that future person. Nor would it make sense to assume any clan or family responsibility either, since the fifteen others are unknown. The anonymity and multiplication of ancestors with each generation obscures and dilutes responsibility. Provision for the future becomes more and more a public good as we consider a more and more distant future.

Most people do not take any individual actions on behalf of their descendants beyond grandchildren. From this fact it is sometimes inferred that it is the revealed common will that no consideration for the future beyond two generations is warranted, and that conservation for the distant future is contrary to the public will. This, of course, is a false inference. Even if everyone felt a strong moral obligation to the distant future, he or she would be foolish to try to fulfil that obligation by individual action, for the reason just given – that anonymity and multiplication of ancestors make provision for the distant future a public good. Public goods must be supplied by collective arrangements. The market system of individualistic maximizing behaviour cannot provide public goods, and since provision for the distant future is a public good, sensible people seek it through collective community arrangements, not as individual maximizers.

A further point can be made. My great-great grandchild may also be your great-great grandchild. Therefore, to the extent that I care for my great-great grandchild, I should also care for you and for every other potential progenitor from whom my descendant will inherit, for good or for ill, as much as he or she will inherit from me. The duty of brotherhood among people in the present generation does not rest on this consideration alone, by any means.[3] Rather, this is an additional dimension of brotherhood – the recognition of 'potential co-grand-parenthood' with all people of the present generation. This point is important because concern for the future is often seen as blunting or diverting our ethical concern away from the more pressing problems of present injustice. Considered logically, however, moral concern for the distant future should strengthen rather than weaken the bonds of brotherhood in the present, because we are all potential co-progenitors of each other's descendants.

In the opposite temporal direction, increased moral respect for ancestors should also have the effect of increasing the perception of widespread kinship among members of the present generation. Yet, there is the significant difference that when looking backward at ancestors, current kinship is known; when looking forward, kinship, or rather co-progenitorship, is unknown, and therefore it is harder to exclude anyone or any group because the requisite information for exclusion does not yet exist. Everyone is a potential co-progenitor. Yet, exclusion does take place. We tend to form social classes and promote marriage within the class. This is a denial of potential co-progenitorhood (one dimension of brotherhood) to the excluded class.

The net thrust of these intergenerational considerations is toward community and away from individualism, a thrust generally resisted by the Chicago School. To avoid this thrust and keep the world safe for individualistic utility maximization, Becker and Tomes are driven to the incredible extreme of assuming that people reproduce asexually, like sponges! The reader is encouraged to believe that this assumption is for analytical convenience only and that nothing important hinges on it, because it supposedly can be substituted by the alternative and less absurd assumption of perfect assortative mating, without affecting the analysis. But, as we shall see, this is not the case. The analysis is strongly affected because the definition of the basic decision-making unit must be changed.

If people reproduced asexually, then there would be no exponential fanning out of ancestry: a 'family' would simply be an individual indefinitely extended in time. One could then speak of maximizing the (discounted) utility function of the temporally extended 'family' in the context of individualistic market institutions, because the decision-making maximizing unit would retain its well-defined identity and independence over time. But with sexual reproduction we have the merging of family lines so that decision-making units are neither self-identical nor independent over time; quite the opposite. Consequently, as we have already seen, provision for the distant future becomes a public good.

But what of the claim that the assumption of asexual reproduction can be easily dropped, assuming instead perfect assortative mating? This means that everyone mates with his or her financial and social image or equal. In other words, everyone marries within his or her own class, where each wealth category constitutes a separate class. In effect, the *class* replaces the family as the self-identical unit over time in whose interest maximizing decisions are made. Instead of an individual reproducing without mingling his identity with that of other individuals (asexually), we now have a class reproducing (sexually) but without mingling its identity with the other classes (perfect assortative mating). Potential co-progenitorhood becomes greatly narrowed, and the bonds of community are weakened within the present generation. Thus Becker and Tomes save the formal structure of their model when the assumption of asexual reproduction is replaced by perfect assortative mating, but only by implicitly redefining their basic decision-making unit as a social class rather than an 'infinitely long-lived family'. It should cause some cognitive dissonance to Chicago School individualists to proclaim a model that in effect (if not intention) affirms the social class as the basic self-identical maximizing unit over time! They also have the logical alternative of assuming sexual but incestuous reproduction. This alternative was not considered.

The assumption of asexual reproduction is so wildly counterfactual that, were it really necessary to their model (as in fact it is), it would constitute a *reductio ad absurdum* of the model (as in fact it does). Therefore, it is crucial for Becker and Tomes to argue that the assumption is not really necessary. But if it is not necessary, why make it? It does not simplify by abstracting from the incidental, but obfuscates by abstracting from the fundamental. If the assumption of perfect assortative mating is so obviously equivalent, why not make it from the outset and base the analysis on it rather than just appealing to it in the last act as a vague *deus ex machina*? The answer is that perfect assortative mating actually implies the abandonment of the individualistic model and substitution of the social class as the intergenerational decision-making unit, thereby making irrelevant all theorems and 'results' derived with the assumption of the temporally extended individual ('family') as the decision-making unit. If one wants a world of individualistic maximization on the intergenerational time scale (Chicago School), then one cannot have sexual reproduction. If one opts for sexual reproduction (and how can we do otherwise?), then one must go beyond individualism and recognize community or at least social class as fundamental in matters intergenerational. Becker and Tomes cannot have it both ways.

In conclusion, one is reminded of John Ruskin's satire on the economists of his day.[4] He likened economics to a science of gymnastics which assumes that men have no skeletons. On that assumption, the student gymnast could be rolled up into a ball, flattened out into a cake, and then stretched into a cable, after which the skeleton could be reinserted, with only 'minor' modifications and inconveniences to the student's constitution. Since the emergence of sexual reproduction is evolutionarily prior to the emergence of skeletons, we may conclude either that reality has at last exceeded satire, or that evolutionary economics, Chicago style, requires that evolution reverse its course.

Notes

1. Gary S. Becker and Nigel Tomes, 'An Equilibrium Theory of the Distribution of Income and Intergenerational Mobility', *Journal of Political Economy*, **87** (1979), pp. 1153–89.
2. This, of course, cannot be true for n greater than some definite N, since it would imply more ancestors than there were people alive at that time. This means that we are all distantly related, a point which would reinforce the argument to be made, but which is such a commonplace that I will only point to it in passing.
3. Brotherhood is a value-laden concept, but certainly no more so than individualism. Since Becker and Tomes offer no ethical defence of individualism, I do not feel it incumbent on me to do so for brotherhood, the more so since it does not bear on my main argument anyway.
4. See John Ruskin, *Unto This Last*, edited and with an introduction by Lloyd J. Hubenka (Lincoln: University of Nebraska Press, 1967 [1860]), p. 3.

V On globalization as growth economics' last gasp

Introduction

The last thing the United Nations Conference on Environment and Development (UNCED, Rio, 1994) wanted on their agenda was the issue of free trade and free capital mobility. Environmental issues were controversial enough by themselves. The hope was that the Third World could become rich enough to clean up its environment. The way to become rich was through export-led growth – growing into the US market, without a thought being given to the consequences for the US working class of absorbing Third World exports (in addition to absorbing Japan's exports). Chapter 15 was my unsuccessful effort to put that issue on the agenda.

The review in Chapter 16 of Dani Rodrik's *Has Globalization Gone Too Far?* praises Rodrik for having the courage to defect from the establishment's party line on free trade, while criticizing him for not going further. He is not yet prepared to answer his titular question in the affirmative. But let it be said that Rodrik has been more successful than I was in getting a debate started.

Since globalization is such a current and confused issue, a few more general words of introduction are in order, especially a distinction between globalization and internationalization.

Internationalization refers to the increasing importance of international trade, international relations, treaties, alliances, and so on. *Inter*national, of course, means between or among nations. The basic unit remains the nation, even as relations among nations become increasingly necessary and important as they try to grow into each other's markets and ecological space, as well as into the global commons. *Globalization* refers to global economic integration of many fomerly national economies into one global economy, mainly by free trade and free capital mobility, but also by easy or uncontrolled migration. Globalization is the effective erasure of national boundaries for economic purposes. What was international becomes interregional. What was governed by comparative advantage becomes governed by absolute advantage. What was many becomes one. The very word 'integration' derives from 'integer', meaning one, complete, or whole. Integration is the act of combining into one whole. Since there can be only one whole, only one unity with reference to which parts are integrated, it follows that global economic integration logically implies national economic disintegration. By disintegration I do not mean that the productive plant of each country is annihilated, but rather that its parts are torn out of their national context (dis-integrated), in order to be re-integrated into the new whole, the globalized economy. As the saying goes, to make an omelette you have to break some eggs. The disintegration of the national egg is necessary to integrate the global omelette.

Many people celebrate globalization. I lament and oppose it because I think the nation, for all its faults, remains the primary locus of community in a world of increasingly licentious and large-scale corporate individualism to which globalization gives free rein. As nations cease to be separate, loosely connected units, and become nodes in a tightly integrated global network, as their boundaries lose economic significance, then do we really need to defend them? We will presumably no longer need customs officials or border guards. But what about the military proper? What precisely are they going to defend in a globalized world? The globe is not under threat of invasion. Do we imagine that national boundaries will long retain any political or cultural significance once their economic significance is gone?

Can the industrial part of the military–industrial complex globalize while the military part remains national? With the global mobility of capital comes the mobility of both the industrial base and the tax base that support the national military. Is not national defence a social good, just like welfare or environmental protection? Will not globalization undercut a nation's ability to tax mobile capital to support its military, just as it undercuts a nation's ability to tax capital to support welfare and environmental programmes? What's the big difference?

No doubt it is considerations such as these that lead some people to favour globalization. It is good, in their view, precisely because it makes the national military obsolete, along with the rest of the nation state. But while globalization seems to make national militaries obsolete, it does not, unfortunately, remove the need for appeal to force. Laws, contracts and property rights still must exist and be enforced, even if they are global rather than national. Economic inequality and class conflict grow as the old national social contract between capital and labour dissolves, along with the power of nations to guarantee it. Do the globalizers envisage a global government to enforce global laws with a global police force? Or do we, to avoid really big government, follow the privatization and deregulation model all the way, letting the military evolve into private Pinkerton guards hired by each global corporation to protect its property and enforce its contracts?

I know that we have not arrived at this point yet. But make no mistake about the fact that globalization is being pushed hard by powerful transnational corporations, and that the weakening of the nation is part of the agenda. Maybe globalization will stop before it completely disintegrates nations. But who or what will stop it? US politicians, their academic advisers, and the politically correct thought police ritually dismiss any opposition to globalization by chanting the 'x-word' – xenophobia. President Clinton, often criticized for not standing for anything, has in fact stood quite firmly for globalization.

15 Free trade, sustainable development and growth: some serious contradictions – a review*

This chapter is a great disappointment. It is the unison snoring of supine economists in deep dogmatic slumber. There are no new thoughts, and many old ideas, such as comparative advantage, are totally misunderstood. The theme is 'promoting development through trade', but the thrust is to promote international trade and global economic integration as self-evidently good, and then call the result 'development' – even worse, call it *'sustainable* development' in the hope that chanting this mantra will free us from the obligation to define it, and absolve us from our addiction to robbing the future. Below are some reasons for my disappointment. One who has been awakened likes to awaken others, especially if the house is on fire. Hence the sometimes shrill tone of this review.

The first principle listed under the subtitle 'basis for action' is: 'An open trading system, which leads to the distribution of global production in accordance to comparative advantage, is of benefit to all trading partners.' Everything that follows is based on this premise. Unfortunately the principle of comparative advantage rests on the assumption that capital is immobile between nations. As David Ricardo clearly explained, if capital could cross national boundaries, then it would seek absolute advantage (profitability), just as it does within a nation. Only if capital is not free to cross national boundaries in pursuit of absolute advantage is there any reason for it to specialize within the nation, according to the principle of comparative advantage. By logic every country must have a comparative advantage in something, so it could be plausibly argued that trade and specialization guided by comparative advantage would be to the benefit of all trading partners. But there is no reason why each country must have an absolute advantage in some-

* This review of the draft Section I, Chapter I of the United Nations Conference on Environment and Development (UNCED) Agenda 21 (International Policies to Accelerate Sustainable Development in Developing Countries and Related Domestic Policies) was prepared at the invitation of the Centre for Our Common Future as input to PrepCom IV held in New York City in March 1992. These comments relate only to that draft chapter. The views presented here are those of the author and should in no way be attributed to the World Bank. Reprinted in *Population and Environment*, **14** (4), March 1993, pp. 439–43.

thing, and thus no guarantee that specialization and trade according to absolute advantage will not harm one of the trading countries. As capital leaves a country in pursuit of greater absolute advantage, then that country loses both capital and jobs and becomes worse off. In today's world nothing could be clearer than that capital is highly mobile internationally, often electronically, with the speed of light. However valid comparative advantage may be as a logical exercise, it is irrelevant in a world dominated by international mobility of capital in pursuit of absolute advantage. There may be good arguments for free trade, but, in a world of international capital mobility, comparative advantage *cannot* be one of them. The confident assertion that an open trading system will benefit all trading partners is utterly unfounded.

There is an obvious conflict between an international policy of free trade and a national policy of internalization of external environmental costs (both advocated in the chapter). A country which internalizes environmental costs into its prices will be at a disadvantage in free trade with a country that does not internalize environmental costs. Therefore, national protection of a basic policy of internalization of environmental costs constitutes a clear justification for tariffs on imports from a country which does not internalize its environmental costs. This is not 'protectionism' in the usual sense of protecting an inefficient industry, but rather *it is the protection of an efficient national policy of internalization of environmental costs!* Agenda 21 cannot see the difference. Economists argue that trade restrictions are a 'second-best' policy for achieving environmental ends. True enough, but the problem is that the 'first-best' policy of domestic internalization of environmental costs will be undercut internationally if not protected by a cost-equalizing tariff.

There is no mention of the problem of trade in toxic wastes – should such trade be carried out on the principle of comparative advantage, and toxics sent abroad, probably to the Third World, or should toxic wastes be internalized to their country of origin on the principle that the best way to internalize the risks of any enterprise is to have the owners live next to it?

The chapter urges the reduction of tariffs in developing countries on all products of export interest to developing countries – without the slightest consideration of the consequences for the working class of the developed countries! There is at least some truth in the old saying that foreign aid is the transfer of money from poor people in the rich countries to rich people in poor countries, and it ought to be taken more seriously. The idea that the working class of developed countries should enter into direct competition with the low-wage masses of the

Third World is quite popular among capitalists in the industrial countries. International capital mobility, coupled with free trade of products, stimulates an international standards-lowering competition to attract capital: wages can be lowered, as can health insurance, worker safety standards, environmental standards, and so on all in the name of reducing costs. But reducing costs by increasing efficiency, and reducing costs by lowering standards are two very different things. Avoiding standards-lowering competition requires more than 'free trade'.

If by wise policy or blind luck a country has managed to control its population growth, provide social insurance, high wages, reasonable working hours, and other benefits to its working class (that is, the large majority of its citizens), should it really allow these benefits to be competed down to the world average in the name of 'free trade'? So-called free trade might more accurately be called 'deregulated international commerce' to emphasize its affinity with other recent experiences with deregulation, such as savings and loan institutions, and junk-bond-financed leveraged buyouts. Developed country capitalists have generously offered to share the wages of the working classes of their countries with the poor of the world. This gesture is only made more generous by the prospect that the levelling of wages will be completely downward due to the vast number and rapid growth rate of underemployed populations in the Third World. The idea that growth will raise world wages to the current rich country level, and that all can consume resources at the US per capita rate, is a wishful thought that is in total conflict with ecological limits that are already stressed beyond sustainability. Growth for the poor is indeed necessary, but without making ecological room for it by a reduction in growth of resource consumption by the rich, and a reduction in population growth of both rich and poor, it cannot happen. Agenda 21 hides its face from these problems!

Even though the working class in the North is supposed to be willing to sacrifice its high-wage jobs in the name of free trade, the idea is that the North as a whole (mainly the capitalist class) must consume ever more to provide the markets for Third World products and raw materials. Import substitution is considered inefficient while export is considered efficient, almost by definition. There is no recognition of the wisdom of relative self-sufficiency in basic foods. Would it not make more sense for the Third World countries to transform their own resources into products needed by their own people, rather than export them to the North in exchange for consumer goods for Southern élites?

In paragraph 15 we are told that international trade promotes growth, which gives additional resources for environmental improvement, and that a sound environment provides the resources to sustain growth and underpin a continuing expansion of trade, which again promotes growth ... and so on, evidently a self-reinforcing spiral without limit. And this is what they (ingenuously or deviously?) call *'sustainable* development'! Nowhere is there any recognition that in fact the economy is an open subsystem of an ecosystem which is closed, finite and non-growing. Nowhere is there any recognition that sustainability requires that growth must not exceed the capacity of the larger system to regenerate resources and absorb wastes at sustainable rates and without disrupting other vital natural services, such as photosynthesis, nitrogen fixation, and so on.

The best thing one can say about the chapter is that there is at least a timid recommendation that the excessive burden of debt service on Third World countries should be reduced. However, this is to be *without* reducing the flow of new lending to the same countries! While advocacy of debt reduction is good, it is distressing that the system of deregulated international commerce (free trade) that gave rise to these unrepayable unsustainable debts is so uncritically embraced as the key to future 'sustainable' development.

Nowhere is there any recognition that although trade will allow some countries to live beyond the ecological carrying capacity of their borders, all countries cannot possibly do this – no matter how much world trade may expand, all countries cannot be net importers of raw materials and natural services. Thus the experience of The Netherlands or Hong Kong cannot be generalized. Free trade allows the ecological burden to be spread more evenly across the globe, thereby buying time before facing up to limits, but at the cost of eventually having to face the problem simultaneously and globally rather than sequentially and nationally.

In conclusion, I would urge the authors of this chapter to read J.M. Keynes's essay on 'National Self-Sufficiency', from which this closing thought is taken:

> I sympathize therefore, with those who would minimize, rather than those who would maximize, economic entanglement between nations. Ideas, knowledge, art, hospitality, travel – these are the things which should of their nature be international. But let goods be homespun whenever it is reasonably and conveniently possible; and, above all, let finance be primarily national.

It is clear that the authors of Agenda 21 are among those who would maximize economic entanglement between nations. Why? Because they believe that unentangled nations are incompetent to manage their own affairs without the expert tutelage of multinational corporations and multilateral development agencies. They also believe that trade promotes growth, growth helps the environment, the environment helps growth, which in turn helps trade which then helps growth again. This spiraling positive feedback loop is their vision of '*sustainable* development'. They have missed the point of the whole discussion.

16 Review of Dani Rodrik's *Has Globalization Gone Too Far?* (Institute for International Economics, 1997)

After reading the Preface by C. Fred Bergsten, Director of the Institute for International Economics which published the book, I very nearly stopped reading. That would have been a mistake, because Rodrik's book is in fact very good – it taught me many things, and I will certainly recommend it to students and colleagues. What turned me off in Bergsten's Preface was his eagerness to assure the reader that Rodrik 'clearly answers the question posed in the title of this book in the negative . . .'. Ho-hum, I thought – one more boring, snoring recitation of the virtues of comparative advantage from the free trade establishment. But for some reason I read on, and discovered that while Rodrik does not in fact answer the titular question directly, much less clearly, the unmistakable thrust of his argumentation is that globalization has been vastly oversold by economists (including his patron, the Institute for International Economics).

The closest thing we get to a direct answer is: 'So has international economic integration gone too far? Not if policy makers act wisely and imaginatively' (p. 9). Have I gone too far in drinking this stimulating poison? Not if I have a wise physician with an imaginative antidote! But Rodrik does not claim to be the wise physician, nor to have an antidote. And on occasion he seems to recognize that there is no antidote. I suggest that the right answer to the titular question, and the one most supported by Rodrik's own arguments, is: yes, globalization has gone too far in that we are paying an underestimated cost in national disintegration for an exaggerated benefit from global integration. But Rodrik is not (yet?) willing to say this in so many words, even though it seems clear that is what he means.

The main argument of the book, Rodrik tells us, is

> that the most serious challenge for the world economy in the years ahead lies in making globalization compatible with domestic social and political stability – or to put it even more directly, in ensuring that international economic integration does not contribute to domestic social disintegration. (p. 2)

Yet Rodrik does a very good job of showing that domestic social disintegration is a direct consequence of global economic integration. On p. 64, after much careful argument, he summarizes:

> Hence the evidence suggests three things: globalization reduces the ability of governments to spend resources on social programs, it makes it more difficult to tax capital, and labor now carries a growing share of the tax burden . . .

With that kind of economic disintegration can social disintegration be far behind?

Global economic integration logically implies national economic disintegration. To integrate means to organize around a single unifying principle – to arrange parts into a single structured whole. When particular economic activities are integrated into a national whole, then the nation is the basic organic unity, and the globe is a loose federation of nations (a world in which classical comparative advantage makes sense). Alternatively, when basic economic activities are integrated into a single global economy, then nations are no longer structured wholes but just vestigial lines on the map of a new cosmopolitan world in which resource allocation follows absolute advantage. For globalization to happen the basic pieces have to be rearranged – torn out of one integrating context and recombined into another. If we opt for global economic integration we are simultaneously opting for national economic disintegration. That much is just logic. The remaining question, a factual one, is: does economic disintegration of a nation result in its social disintegration? I think it clearly does, and Rodrik at times seems to agree, but in the end seems to think that we can square the circle by appealing to *virtu, fortuna* and political imagination. But Rodrik himself seems unable to imagine anything other than globalization of one stripe or another.

Rodrik sees three sources of tension between globalization and society.

First, groups that can cross national boundaries are benefited at the expense of those that cannot. Capitalists and many professionals benefit; labourers lose. Globalization both lowers the demand for unskilled labour and makes that demand more elastic, thus reducing both labour's *ex post* income and *ex ante* bargaining power.

Second, globalization engenders conflicts between nations over basic norms (child labour laws, environmental and safety standards, and so on) and the social institutions and practices based on those norms. GATT and WTO notwithstanding, most people attach value to processes as well as products and outcomes.

Third, provision of social insurance by governments has been undercut by free trade and free capital mobility. Mobile capital can escape social welfare taxes, leaving labour to pay, either by higher taxes or lower benefits. Interestingly, Rodrik argues that the more open an economy, the more likely it is to be a welfare state. The welfare state is part of a social contract in which the greater risks to citizens of a more open economy are compensated by a larger safety net. Ironically the very welfare system that provided the social insurance required to induce citizens to accept the extra risks of global integration is now being undercut by globalization itself, principally by capital mobility. Rodrik asks 'What if, by reducing the civic engagement of internationally mobile groups, globalization loosens the civic glue that holds societies together and exacerbates social fragmentation?' (p. 70). An excellent question! But why pretend that we don't know the answer?

On p. 31 we are told that 'Opening up to international trade is formally equivalent, in all economic respects, to technological progress.' If we are willing to accept some redistribution in order to get a larger pie from technical progress, then why not the same for trade liberalization? He then says *'This, I believe, is the central argument in favor of maintaining open borders to international commerce.'* But if this really is the 'central argument', it is surprisingly easy to counter, and Rodrik himself effectively uses it to cut the other way:

> Since governments routinely interfere in deciding what kind of technologies are permissible domestically, so as to take into account social costs or national norms, it is difficult to make a hard-line case as to why international trade should be categorically exempt from this same kind of approach. (p. 48)

More generally in a footnote on p. 36 Rodrik proclaims that 'National sovereignty implies the ability of each country to sever its trade links with others if the trade undermines its sovereign choices at home.' Bravo! As an example, I offer the following: a sovereign country decides on a high-wage development policy, which leads it to limit its population growth and limit its income inequality. This country is not obligated to undermine its own high-wage policy by integrating through free trade and capital mobility with countries that have chosen a low-wage policy based on high population growth and very unequal distribution of income. Yet on p. 76 when presented with a similar position stated by an American Federation of Labor–Congress of Industrial Organizations representative, Rodrik complains that limiting trade with low-wage countries is a cardinal sin against comparative advantage and is therefore wicked!

While there are frequent references to comparative advantage, nowhere is there a recognition that the argument of comparative advantage is premised on capital immobility between nations. Rodrik should either advocate restrictions on international capital mobility if he wants to keep the world safe for comparative advantage, or base his arguments for free trade only on absolute advantage if he wants to keep capital mobile. Like most free traders he does neither.

Nevertheless, compared to your average trade theorist, Rodrik is truly a breath of fresh air. This is not to damn him with faint praise – in absolute terms his book is insightful, honest and scholarly – but with lapses. One scholarly lapse is his failure to cite others who have already made similar arguments. He goes no further in this direction than briefly discussing William Greider's *One World Ready or Not*, but mainly as an example of 'popular confusion'. The other lapse, already evident from what has been said, is that he pulls his punches. This may be understatement resulting from admirable scholarly humility, or perhaps it is due to a failure of nerve. More likely it reflects an intermediate stage in Rodrik's own intellectual evolution. I get the feeling that he is almost halfway to a rejection of globalization, but is being held back by influences from the company he keeps. However, Rodrik was courageous enough to bait the lions of free trade in their own den, and that deserves respect, because the lions may not forgive him. With friends like Rodrik, globalization cannot survive many enemies. I wish him well.

VI   On money

Introduction

Under our present fractional reserve banking system some 95 per cent of our money supply is created by the private banking sector. That money is loaned into existence on the condition that it be paid back with interest. In other words, money is created in such a way that its very existence pushes the economy to grow. Money created by fractional reserve banking is not neutral with respect to growth – it is a growth pusher. For all those loans to be paid back with interest the borrower must make the money grow by a rate at least as high as the rate of interest. Back when it was thought that growth was always good, that uneconomic growth was impossible, such a monetarily induced growth bias was considered advantageous. But as uneconomic growth has become the relevant danger an extra growth push from the money supply has become a disadvantage. In addition to pushing growth, fractional reserve banking reinforces both booms and depressions, making the economy more unstable than it would be with a more constant money supply controlled by the state as a public service. Failure to grow leads to a contraction of the money supply, which makes it still more difficult to grow, and so on. In the 1920s and 1930s some of the leading economists in the USA (Irving Fisher, Frank Knight, Henry Simons) argued forcefully against fractional reserve banking on the grounds that it was a source of instability and an unwarranted subsidy to the private banking sector. This debate has all but disappeared from academic economics as well as from the political agenda, even while global financial volatility due to free international capital mobility has made it all the more important. Financial transactions have expanded far more rapidly than real transactions, thus increasing the importance of the financial sector and the dangers of fractional reserve banking.

17 Money, debt and wealth*

Introduction

Money ranks with the wheel and fire among ancient inventions without which the modern world could not have come into being. But it is much more mysterious. It is a unit of account that changes size like a rubber yardstick; a store of value that can swell or shrink over time; a medium of exchange that often never leaves the bank; an interest-bearing debt and a non-interest-bearing debt; a commodity (like gold) and a non-commodity token (paper money); easily transferable into real assets by individuals yet not at all transferable into real assets by the community; counterfeiters are sent to jail for making it, but the private banking system can create it out of nothing and lend it at interest; some economists think it merely a veil behind which real factors determine economic life, others consider it among the most important of determinants; some think its quantity should be determined by a fixed rule, others that it should be manipulated by public authorities; and in addition, some people even claim that it inspires a love that is the root of all evil. At least it is a rich source of bewilderment and danger. Probably in today's world more people are hurt by out-of-control money than by out-of-control wheels and fires.

Money in the exponential-growth culture

Our national institutions governing money and finance are embedded in a culture which has come to accept exponential growth as the norm. Although real wealth cannot grow exponentially for long, our cultural symbol and measure of wealth, money, may indeed grow both exponentially and indefinitely. This lack of symmetry in behaviour between the reality measured and the measuring rod has serious consequences.

Exponential growth has the characteristic of a fixed doubling time. The classic example of placing one grain of wheat on the first square of a chessboard, two on the second, four on the third, and so on, leads to the last or 64th square alone containing 2^{63} grains, or about 1000 times the world's annual wheat crop. The board as a whole would contain twice that amount, or 2^{64} grains. As M. King Hubbert put it,

---

* Modified Afterword from Herman E. Daly and John B. Cobb, Jr, *For the Common Good: Redirecting the Economy toward community, the environment, and a sustainable future*, 2nd edition, Beacon Press, 1994, pp. 407–42.

the world will not tolerate 64 doublings of even a grain of wheat. If the present human population had begun with a single couple, there could not have been more than about 31 doublings. At 46 doublings we would have a population density of one person per square metre over the earth. Hubbert concluded that the maximum number of doublings of any single biological population or industrial product is on the order of a few tens. And if many biological populations and stocks of industrial goods must double simultaneously, as is the case for an exponentially growing economy, then even a few tens is too many doublings. Clearly Hubbert was right to view 'exponential growth as a transient phenomenon in human history'. Nevertheless, as Hubbert (1976) also pointed out,

> during the last two centuries we have known nothing but exponential growth and in parallel we have evolved what amounts to an exponential-growth culture, a culture so heavily dependent on the continuance of exponential growth for its stability that it is incapable of reckoning with problems of non-growth.

What are the features of this exponential culture? The custom of discounting future values to arrive at an equivalent present value is simply the compound interest calculation run in reverse. But we are more accustomed to running the calculation forward to see how much money we have to set aside to support us in old age. Without exponential growth how can we meet pension fund payments, and insurance claims whose actuarial calculation assumed growth? How can the poor get better off, and the rich too, without growth? How can the national deficit be reduced without increased taxes or reduced government spending, unless we can 'grow the economy', as politicians are now putting it? And how can we maintain full employment unless we stimulate investment? And does not investment mean growth? Are we not truly trapped in an exponential-growth culture?

Marx (1867) argued that the exponential growth culture was a necessary part of capitalism. His historical analysis relates the growth culture to money in the following way. Barter, the exchange of one commodity for a different commodity, symbolized as $C-C^*$, is the simplest and oldest method of exchange. One person has C and prefers C^*; another has C^* and prefers C. Both are better off after the trade, although no new physical production has occurred. The use value to both individuals has increased, but the exchange value is irrelevant. Barter can be mutually beneficial, but the necessary coincidence of wants severely limits its extent.

That limit is overcome by the use of money as a medium of exchange. This gives rise to what Marx called simple commodity production, symbolized by $C-M-C^*$. Here money functions to overcome barter's problem of requiring a coincidence of wants. But the focus is still on increasing the use value to each individual. Exchange value, the sum of money M, is entirely instrumental to bringing about the increase in use value by facilitating the exchange of commodities which are exchanged only for the purpose of increasing use values. The process begins and ends with a commodity use value.

The critical change comes in the next historical step, which Marx called capitalist circulation, symbolized by $M-C-M^*$. The object is no longer the increase of use value, but the expansion of exchange value in money. $M^*-M = dM$, and dM must grow. An initial capital, M, is used to hire labour and buy raw materials which are then turned into a commodity C, which in turn is sold for a greater amount of money, M^*.

The shift of focus from use value to exchange value is crucial. Commodity accumulation and use values, C, are self-limiting. Fifty hammers are not much better than two (one and a spare) as far as use value is concerned. But if we turn our focus to exchange value, then fifty hammers are much better than two, and better yet if available as fifty hammers' worth of fungible money.

The exchange value of commodities in general, abstracted in money, becomes the focus of accumulation. There is nothing to limit how much abstract exchange value one can own. Unlike concrete use values, which spoil or deteriorate when hoarded (due to entropy), abstract exchange value can accumulate indefinitely without spoilage or storage costs. In fact abstract exchange value grows by itself, earning interest, and then interest on the interest. Marx, and Aristotle before him, pointed out the danger in this 'money fetishism', which is a particular case of the general fallacy of misplaced concreteness.

In our own time this historical process of abstracting farther away from use value has perhaps been carried to the limit in the so-called 'paper economy', which might be symbolized as $M-M^*$, the direct conversion of money into more money without reference to commodities even as an intermediate step. Of course this has long been with us in the form of money in the bank growing at interest. But the scope for money making through tax avoidance, mergers, takeovers, 'greenmail', and all forms of insider trading has increased the apparent ability of money to expand with little reference to use value – indeed, sometimes by the destruction of use values, induced by a tax code that itself confuses wealth with debt – for example, tax-free interest on junk bonds used to finance leveraged buyouts.

The objective of takeovers, as explained by William Greider (1989), is

> to extract the capital invested in the underutilized real assets of the corporation so that the money could be redeployed in higher yielding financial instruments. It is another dramatic example of how finance has triumphed over the real economy. Why own a factory when your capital will draw a better real return from paper?

But as Greider goes on to point out, the fundamental driving force behind the takeovers was the high level of real interest rates in the 1980s. If the real assets embodied in an enterprise could not earn a return that matched the high interest rate, the incentive was to convert the enterprise into cash by disassembling it and selling it off, and investing the money in paper earning the high interest rate.

Of course all investments are in competition with the interest rate and if they cannot produce a higher yield they should, by the rule of efficiency, be liquidated and the capital invested in some alternative that does beat the interest rate.[1] This supposes that the interest rate itself reflects a kind of marginal real rate of return on capital. But that is only one factor underlying the interest rate, which also reflects monetary policy, balance of payments policy, concern or lack thereof for the future, expectations about the future, both rational and irrational, monopoly power, the pattern of subsidies and penalties in the tax code, and so on. When these other factors drive the interest rate up, real assets will be cannibalized and reassembled in faster-growing alternatives, just as exploited species will be driven to extinction when their biological growth rate at all population levels falls short of the interest rate, and their place in the sun taken by a faster-growing species. But where are the real investments that will earn more than the old assets, and will they earn enough more to pay for the social cost of displaced labourers, disrupted pensions and medical insurance, and dissolved communities? And if these new investments are so obvious, why would not businessmen see them and invest in them in the normal course of affairs? Why do we need lawyers, brokers and accountants to accelerate the process, especially when these people have absolutely no knowledge of either the technological production processes or social community relations that are being disrupted wholesale by their remote financial activities? And when most of them make money on the deal even if it turns out to be a public disaster, we seem to have a considerable potential for 'moral hazard', the economist's term for a case in which the costs of imprudent risk taking are borne by someone other than the risk taker – a concept we will have further occasion to employ.

Kenneth Boulding makes a helpful distinction between assets which are 'used up' and those which are 'worn out'. Some things must be used up in order to yield their service – food and fuel, for example. Other things are not necessarily degraded in the act of use – they wear out over time, but their wearing out is an incidental, even if unavoidable, consequence of the service they render in use. For example, human bodies, capital equipment and durable consumer goods all wear out, but could yield their service even if they did not wear out. But gasoline or food, for example, can only yield their services in the act of being used up. These two forms of assets are complementary – the stock of productive machinery needs a flow of energy to animate it, and the flow of energy needs material stocks through which it can be channelled to satisfy human purposes. The human body needs food to animate and maintain it, but food is worthless without the capital stock of human bodies able to use it for life purposes.

Throughout most of history the flow of energy was revenue from the sun, annually captured by plants. Like manna from heaven it was renewed every day, but could not be accumulated for future use except within narrow limits. The world is usually only one harvest away from starvation. With the discovery of fossil fuels, stored sunshine from the distant past has become available. But we cannot use it directly to feed our internal metabolic fire – that must still be fed by sunlight captured by plants, although the plants' ability to capture sunlight can be increased by fertilizers made with fossil fuels. We use fossil fuel to feed the external fires of machines that lighten our labour. But fossil fuels are destined to be used up, and what Frederick Soddy (1926) called the 'flamboyant period' based on their use will come to an end.

Although it is possible to accumulate capital for the future, this process is limited by the complementarity of the stock (permanent wealth that gets worn out) with the annual revenue (perishable wealth that gets used up) needed to animate it and maintain it. As the stock grows larger so does its annual depreciation. The maintenance deductions from the future revenue will grow, as will the amount required to run the larger capital stock (human bodies, livestock, machines). The fixed flow of sunlight and the resulting renewable but perishable revenue will prove to be the limiting factor in the accumulation of wealth, since it is the least subject to accumulation and expansion, and its complementarity with the stock of permanent wealth limits the expansion of the latter.

The main point, however, is that the growth of wealth is physically limited while the growth of debt is not. The exact biophysical sequence through which the former limits work themselves out is highly interesting, but not the central issue. Whatever the progress of science in discovering new resources and techniques, it could not possibly match the explosive mathematical growth of compound interest.

Aristotle and the Church Fathers, as well as the Jewish and Islamic worlds, have all condemned usury as in some sense 'unnatural'. Aristotle said money is sterile and does not have the physical capacity to reproduce itself like crops and livestock. The problem as we have stated it here is not so much that money is sterile, but that it grows far too rapidly and artificially – mathematically it is hyper-fecund, but physically it is barren, as Aristotle said. Therefore, reasoning about wealth in terms of money can become a massive exercise in the fallacy of misplaced concreteness.

The difference between real wealth and money was noted by Nobel Laureate economist James Tobin (1965, p. 676):

> The community's wealth now has two components: the real goods accumulated through past real investment and fiduciary or paper 'goods' manufactured by the government from thin air. Of course, the nonhuman wealth of such a nation 'really' consists only of its tangible capital. But as viewed by the inhabitants of the nation individually, wealth exceeds the tangible capital stock by the size of what we might term the fiduciary issue. This is an illusion, but only one of the many fallacies of composition which are basic to any economy or society. The illusion can be maintained unimpaired as long as society does not actually try to convert all of its paper wealth into goods.

In the following section we will review the well-known process by which commercial banks are able to play a far larger role than government in manufacturing money out of thin air. However, the basic point stands. To maintain the illusion, not only must society not try to convert all its money into real wealth, but neither must it try to convert all its 'fiduciary issue' into currency – that is, all its interest-bearing private bank debt (not legal tender) into non-interest-bearing government debt (legal tender). Fractional reserve banking requires that a second and more dangerous illusion be maintained.

The culture of exponential growth that now dominates Western society, and increasingly the world as a whole, is not sustainable. To move away from this culture, toward a culture capable of dealing with problems of non-growth, would require us to tie money more closely to real wealth. To see how this might be done we need a clear picture of how money is now created and what it really is. We must understand

how private banks create money, how they acquired that power historically, and what would be necessary to restore that power entirely to the
State.

The creation of money

In general we have an adequate common-sense notion of how real
wealth is created. It requires work that transforms natural resources
and energy into usable goods. The increase of production per worker
requires both the organization of labour in specialized roles and the
introduction of capital and the technology it embodies.

The creation of money, on the other hand, is far less well understood
by the public. Some think, naïvely, that this is primarily a matter of the
government's printing presses. But this applies only to the legal tender
consisting of coins and paper money – a small part of the money that
actually flows through the economy. Most money is the creation of
commercial banks.

Originally, money could be created only by the monarch. As long as
the money was a commodity, such as gold, and its value was regulated
by the real cost of mining gold, the creation of money was simply
the standardization of one commodity as an instrument of exchange.
Beginning in the Middle Ages, even when gold circulated as money,
there was frequently a difference between the monetary value of the
gold coin and the market value of the commodity as gold metal. The
one-ounce gold coin with the monarch's face on it usually had less than
an ounce of gold in it, and to that extent was partially token money.
The profit to the monarch of putting less than an ounce of gold in a
one-ounce gold coin was called seigniorage. It was justified initially as
necessary to defray the expense of coinage, but it was in fact a source
of profit to the Crown arising from its prerogative to issue money.
Seigniorage is the difference between the monetary value of the token
and its commodity value. Today, for paper currency created by the
government, the commodity value is nil, so that seigniorage is nearly
equal to the full monetary value of the paper currency.

The manufacture of money by governments is thus a source of public
income. However, this source is greatly reduced today by the fact that
most money is now created by private banks. Money creation has
become a source of private income. Historically this shift of the money-
creating prerogative evolved with the goldsmith-bankers who accepted
deposits of gold for safekeeping. Transferring ownership claims to gold
in the safe was easier than taking it out and giving it to the other party,
who then put it back on deposit for safekeeping with the goldsmith.
Hence the practice of payment by cheque developed. Experience taught

the goldsmith-banker that most of the gold just sat in the vault, and that only a small fraction needed to be on hand in the till as reserves against day-to-day discrepancies between new deposits and withdrawals. Much of the gold could safely be loaned out at interest. Of course there was always the possibility of a panic or run on the goldsmith-banker, so the practice was not without risk. The goldsmith-bankers in Amsterdam got a law passed making it a hanging offence to start a run on the goldsmith. But one day there was a run, and of course the goldsmith could not pay. The matter was 'resolved', not by hanging the unknown individual who started the run, but by hanging the goldsmith (Barber, 1973).

In spite of such setbacks, the practice of keeping fractional reserves against loans grew, and with that practice banks acquired the power to create money, not in the sense of legal tender, but in the sense of customary means of payment, cheques, accepted in exchange for goods and services. This growth did not depend on any governmental decision. The fact that this practice linked the public function of supplying money with the private activity of lending at interest is a historical happenstance, not the result of legislative design.[2]

Private creation of money by banks evolved long before it was understood. Joseph Schumpeter (1954, p. 1114) claims that, as late as the 1920s, 99 out of 100 economists believed that banks could not create money any more than cloakrooms could create coats. Part of the confusion may have been the distinction between money (customary means of payment), and legal tender (money that one is legally obliged to accept in payment). Banks do not create legal tender; only governments can do that. But banks do create customary means of payment. The difficulty economists had in recognizing this elicits the following comment from Schumpeter:

> This is a most interesting illustration of the inhibition with which analytic advance has to contend and in particular of the fact that people may be perfectly familiar with a phenomenon for ages and even discuss it frequently without realizing its true significance and without admitting it into their general scheme of thought. (Schumpeter, 1954, p. 1115)

Although today the fact that commercial banks create much more money than the government is now explained in every introductory economics text, its full significance and effects on the economy have still not been sufficiently considered. As the nature of money is better understood, it should be possible to develop policies for using it more effectively for the common good.

In an unregulated banking system based on fractional reserves, each bank determines how much reserves it will keep on hand to meet the net demands of its customers for cash. The smaller the reserves, the more can be lent, and the greater the profits of the bank. Consequently, some banks kept insufficient reserves, leading to loss of confidence, a run on the bank, and failure. Many depositors lost their money. To reduce this risk, the USA established the Federal Reserve system which regulates the amount of reserves required and provides extra funds in emergencies. Also the Federal Deposit Insurance Corporation insures depositors against loss of up to $100000, which removes the main reason for runs on banks.

Today bank reserves do not consist of gold or any other commodity, but of cash and the bank's own deposits at the Federal Reserve. Banks are legally required to hold reserves against their demand deposits. The fraction of total demand deposits that must be held as reserves is set by law, currently less than 10 per cent on average. Let the legally required fraction of deposits kept as reserves be r. Then reserves above the requirement are excess reserves, and their fraction is $1-r$.

To give a numerical example, assume that r is 10 per cent, then $(1-r)$ is 90 per cent. Assume that there is only one bank, a monopoly bank. An additional $100 cash deposit (or creation of new reserves of $100 by the Federal Reserve) results in an additional $100 demand deposit credited to the depositor. So far there is no creation of money, just a change from cash to demand deposit in the books of the depositor. But now the monopoly bank has $90 in excess reserves. It can lend out up to $900, creating demand deposits up to that amount in the name of the borrowers. Total additional demand deposits are now $1000, consisting of the $900 new loans and the $100 demand deposit exchanged for the original cash deposit. Additional reserves are $100 (the original cash deposit). The 10 per cent reserve requirement is met; $900 in new money has been created. The monopoly bank can expand its demand deposits by a factor of $1/r = 1/0.1 = 10$ times new reserves, because it knows that all cheques written against these new deposits will be redeposited with it, being the only bank.

If there are many different banks, then each bank must assume that cheques written on its new demand deposits will be deposited to another bank, and that it will quickly lose that amount of reserves in its account at the Federal Reserve, since that cheque will be cleared by transferring reserves from its account to the other bank's account at the Federal Reserve. Remember, the bank's deposits with the Federal Reserve count as reserves. Therefore, in the many-bank case, a single bank receiving an additional $100 cash deposit can only safely lend out its excess reserves, namely $90. But as that $90 is spent it is redeposited by the recipient in another bank. The second bank must keep 10 per cent in reserve, so it has excess reserves of 0.9 ($90) = $81. The $81 is loaned, spent and deposited in a third bank, which then can lend 0.9 ($81) = $72.90, and so on. The result of this process of lending, spending and redepositing is that the whole banking system, consisting of many different banks, ends up multiplying the new reserves by the same factor of $1/r$ as the monopoly bank does.[3] So the banking system, whether a monopoly bank or many banks, has a reserves-to-deposit multiplier of $1/r$. Of course, if we have a 100 per cent reserve requirement, that would mean that $r = 1$, and consequently the deposit multiplier would be $1/r = 1/1 = 1$, which would mean that banks could not create money.

The above summary of money creation by banks is incomplete since we have not yet drawn attention to the parallel process of demand deposit contraction as reserves are lost. Individual banks lose reserves when cheques against it are cleared, and when its customers convert demand deposits into cash. The system as a whole does not lose reserves from cheque clearing, as this is just a transfer of reserves among banks. The system as a whole loses reserves when the general public decides to hold more cash money and less cheque money, and when the Federal Reserve reduces total reserves. A reduction in reserves results in a multiple contraction of bank money. As loans are repaid, the receiving bank acquires reserves in the amount of the principal plus interest. These are excess reserves to the receiving bank, but lost reserves to the paying banks. Lost reserves require a reduction in loans of ten (or $1/r$) times the amount of lost reserves, so money is destroyed by the repayment of loans. If the receiving bank keeps the reserves as excess reserves, the reduction in money would be permanent. However, the receiving bank is in business to lend its excess reserves and will make new loans that will soon recreate the money destroyed by repayment of the old loan. There is a continual process of creation and destruction of bank money, with the supply at any instant being the net result of the two processes. If banks keep fully loaned up (no excess reserves), then the money supply is controlled by the government through setting the reserve requirement and controlling the amount of reserves (cash and deposits of commercial banks at the Federal Reserve).

The bank does not increase its assets by the amount of its creation of new money. This creation is offset by the destruction of new money when loans are paid off. But the bank *is* able to charge interest to the borrower on this created money, and that interest is real revenue that does not disappear when the loan is repaid. It can be converted into real assets. If the commercial banking sector is competitive, as it is, it will pay part of that interest to its depositors in order to attract more deposits and be able to create more money and make more loans. The banking system's (or monopoly bank's) gross profit from the original $100 cash deposit is the difference between the interest received on loans of $900 (newly created money) and interest paid on the original $100 cash deposit. Even if the deposit rate of interest were equal to the loan rate of interest there would be considerable margin for profit. Of course, the loan rate is considerably higher than the deposit rate, increasing the margin substantially.

Virtual wealth
The proposal that money be tied much more closely to real wealth is a radical one. Both to understand it and to develop policies that would implement it require more fundamental thinking about the nature of this elusive entity. But few of those who have reflected profoundly on money and finance have done so with the assumptions developed above: namely, that economics must be about community and is not reducible to individuals, that it has a real biophysical basis and cannot be dealt with only in categories of idealism, and that the fallacy of misplaced concreteness is the cardinal sin of modern economics.

The one economist who thought radically about money and finance from this point of view with great insight was Frederick Soddy (1877–1956). Frederick Soddy is best known not as an economist, but as the 1921 Nobel Laureate in chemistry, honoured for his discovery of the existence of isotopes and general work on radioactive decay with Rutherford.[4] From his own work he was convinced that the atom offered a great potential source of energy for mankind. But he also foresaw its dangers:

> If the discovery were made tomorrow, there is not a nation that would not throw itself heart and soul into the task of applying it to war, just as they are now doing in the case of the newly developed chemical weapons of poison-gas warfare ... If [atomic energy] were to come under existing economic conditions, it would mean the *reductio ad absurdum* of scientific civilization, a swift annihilation ... (Soddy, 1926, p. 28)

Soddy was convinced that there must be something deeply wrong with 'existing economic conditions', with economic thought and institutions, for the gift of scientific knowledge to have become such a threat. Soddy was thus led to a radical critique of economics, which became the central intellectual preoccupation during the latter half of his nearly eighty years. As would be expected of a chemist, he began economic analysis by explaining the bearing of the first and second laws of thermodynamics on economics, anticipating by fifty years the basic ideas of the magisterial work of Georgescu-Roegen, discussed elsewhere in this book. The part of the economy that most caught Soddy's attention, however, was money. Precisely because it was the one measurable quantity that did not obey the laws of thermodynamics, he focused on its role in economic life, and traced most economic problems to its mysteries.

Soddy was dismissed by economists as a 'monetary crank', of the same ilk as Major Douglas or Silvio Gessell. Although he respected these men for having seen the problem, he would have no part in 'funny money' solutions. Indeed, he considered the respected canons of sound banking to be themselves little more than funny money schemes to mystify the public for the enrichment of the bankers and their class. But since Soddy is so often dismissed as a crank it is worth recording the contrary opinion of the celebrated Chicago School economist Frank Knight (1927, p. 732) that Soddy's main book, *Wealth, Virtual Wealth and Debt*, was 'brilliantly written and brilliantly suggestive and stimulating', and further that Soddy's practical theses concerning money were 'highly significant and theoretically correct'.

It is also worth noting that one of Soddy's main proposals, which he called 'pound for pound banking', proposed in 1926, is almost identical to the plan for 100 per cent money put forward by the great American economist Irving Fisher in 1935. But by and large Soddy's economics was an embarrassment to everyone but Soddy. Certainly economists paid it little attention, and fellow chemists thought it a shame that such a brilliant scientist wasted his time on something so far removed from chemistry.

The first step to a proper understanding of money is to return to the fact that money is not wealth; it is no longer even a commodity (like gold or silver). It is a token. A token of what? We are tempted to say a token of wealth, but that is not correct because the value of wealth at any time is much greater than the value of the total stock of money – that is, there are many more coats in the cloakroom than claim tokens. Money is a token of indebtedness – a debt. Money is a form of community or national debt owned by the individual and owed by the community, exchangeable on demand into wealth by voluntary transference to another individual who is willing to part with the wealth in exchange for the money. The value of the total stock of money is not determined by the stock of wealth in existence (or by the flow of new production), but in a curious way by wealth that individuals think exists, but which does not really exist – what Frederick Soddy called 'virtual wealth'.

Virtual wealth is measured by the aggregate value of the real assets that the community voluntarily *abstains* from purchasing in order to hold money instead. In order to escape the inconvenience of barter, everyone must hold money, which could be exchanged by the individual for real wealth, but is not. In Soddy's words (1934, p. 36), 'This aggregate of exchangeable goods and services which the community continuously and permanently goes without (though individual money owners can instantly demand and obtain it from other individuals) the author terms the Virtual Wealth of the community.'

If everyone tried to exchange their money holdings for real assets it could not be done, because all real assets are already owned by someone, and in the final analysis someone has to end up holding the money. So virtual wealth does not really exist over and above the value of all real assets, which is why it is called 'virtual'. Yet people as individuals behave as if virtual wealth were real, because they can easily exchange it for real assets.[5] The aggregate of individuals behaves as if it were richer than the community really is by an amount equal to the virtual wealth of the community. The phenomenon of virtual wealth must occur in a monetary economy, unless the money itself is a commodity – a real asset that circulates at its commodity value. The value of each unit of money is simply the virtual wealth divided by the number of units of money in existence. Virtual wealth varies with the size of population and national income, and the business and payment habits of the community. Since virtual wealth is counted as wealth in determining individual behaviour, but it does not really exist, we are justified in considering it more like debt than like wealth.

Virtual wealth cannot be increased simply by issuing more money, because it is determined by the amount of wealth that the community willingly abstains from holding in order to hold money instead. Issuance of more money tokens than the public is willing to hold will result in their exchanging them for real wealth and driving up the price of real assets to the point where the purchasing power of the larger amount of money is reduced to the amount of real wealth that the community is willing to abstain from holding in order to hold money instead. The value of a dollar's worth of debt depends on how many dollars the value of virtual wealth must be divided among.

Who owns the virtual wealth of the community? It is clearly an artefact of community interdependence and interrelationships. It is owned by individuals, yet since it does not really exist no one owns it. But whoever holds money gave up a real asset for it. The only person who can really exchange virtual wealth for real assets is the issuer of money. Whoever is the creator of the token money, and is the *first* one to put it in circulation by spending or lending it, receives real assets in exchange for tokens. Everyone else has to give up a real asset to get the money that is later given for another real asset. So an amount of real value equal to the virtual wealth is transferred to the issuer of money.

The seigniorage prerogative of the Crown historically has passed, not to the State except marginally, but to the private banking sector, which issues at least nine-tenths of our money. Private bankers are able to lend over 90 per cent of the virtual wealth of the community, which does not really belong to them, and earn interest on it, which does belong to them. Most people would consider that an extraordinarily good deal.

Is it surprising that the institutions that deal in these paper pyramids based on the fallacy of composition should generally try to inspire confidence by giving themselves such names as 'Security, Fidelity, Prudential, Guaranty, Trust ...' corporations? Or that their marble-columned architecture is suggestive of ancient temples, with velvet ropes guiding the faithful to the communion rail where in hushed tones the teller imparts the fiduciary issue? Or that the whole system would have collapsed without the Federal Deposit Insurance Corporation (FDIC)? Indeed, it may now collapse partly because of the FDIC, as banks feel free to play fast and loose with depositors' insured money, and depositors cease being watchdogs since their money is insured. And, to make it much worse, once a bank is 'too big to be allowed to fail', because of the cascading collapse of credit and money that results from holding only a small fraction of deposit liabilities in reserve, the bank's stockholders, as well as depositors, are in effect 'insured' against loss.

It is important to recognize that money and virtual wealth are social phenomena that arise not from mere aggregation of atomistic individuals, but from the community consensus and resulting practical general willingness to accept the agreed-upon token as money. Individuals cannot issue their own money. The essence of money is that it be generally accepted as such within a community, and acceptance of the same monetary standard becomes one of the defining bonds of community.[6] The extent to which virtual wealth should be appropriable by private interests rather than for public use by the nation is an issue that is no longer discussed, but should be.[7] We will return to it. But first, we should look carefully at the confusion between debt and wealth, probably the most important example of the fallacy of misplaced concreteness in economics.

Debt versus wealth

The positive physical quantity two pigs represents wealth that can be seen and touched. But minus two pigs, debt, is an imaginary negative magnitude with no physical dimension. One could as easily have a thousand negative pigs as two. Indeed, according to Soddy, negative numbers were first recognized by Hindu mathematicians for their analogy to debt. Compound interest or exponential growth of negative pigs presents no problem. But exponential growth of positive pigs soon leads to bedlam and ruin.

Given the convenience of owning negative rather than positive pigs, the ruling passion of individuals in a modern economy is to convert wealth into debt in order to derive a permanent future income from it – to convert wealth that perishes into debt that endures, debt that does not rot, costs nothing to maintain, and brings in perennial interest.[8] Individuals cannot amass the physical requirements sufficient for maintenance during their old age, for, like manna, it would rot. Therefore they must convert their non-storable surplus into a lien on future revenue, by letting others consume and invest their surplus now in exchange for the right to share in the increased future revenue.

Although debt can follow the law of compound interest, the real energy revenue from future sunshine, the real future income against which the debt is a lien, cannot grow at compound interest for long. When converted into debt, however, wealth discards its corruptible body to take on an incorruptible one. In so doing debt appears to offer a means of dodging nature, of evading the second law of thermodynamics, the law of randomization, rust and rot. But the idea that all people can live off the interest of their mutual indebtedness is just another perpetual motion scheme – a vulgar delusion on a grand scale.

The perpetual motion delusion of everyone living from interest on debt has arisen, Soddy explains (1926, p. 106),

> Because formerly ownership of land – which, with the sunshine that falls on it, provides a revenue of wealth – secured in the form of rent, a share in the annual harvest without labor or service, upon which a cultured and leisured class could permanently establish itself, the age seems to have conceived the preposterous notion that money, which can buy land, must therefore itself have the same revenue-producing power.

A better example of the fallacy of misplaced concreteness would be hard to find. In a further attempt to elucidate the confusion between wealth and debt, Soddy (1926, p. 103) offers the following:

> Still it might have been apparent that a weight, although it is measured by

what it will pull up, is nevertheless a pull down. The whole idea of balancing one thing against another in order to measure its quantity involves equating the quantity measured against an equal and opposite quantity. Wealth is the positive quantity to be measured and money as the claim to wealth is a debt . . .

The fallacy of composition compounds the errors of misplaced concreteness. Because some people can live on interest it does not follow that all people could. Soddy is arguing that what is obviously impossible for the community must be forbidden in some degree to individuals. If it is not forbidden or at least limited in some way, then at some point the exponentially growing liens of debt-holders will indent the slowly growing future revenue to such an extent that the producers of that revenue will no longer be willing to make such a large transfer, and conflict will result. As Soddy put it (1922, p. 30), 'You cannot permanently pit an absurd human convention, such as the spontaneous increment of debt [compound interest], against the natural law of the spontaneous decrement of wealth [entropy].'

Whatever part of the revenue goes for investment is eventually used up or worn out just as much as is the part that goes directly to consumption. If the investment is productive it will augment the future flow of revenue, but all that exists in the hands of the lender is a lien on that future revenue.[9] Present surplus accumulation can never be changed into future revenue, but only *ex*changed for it under certain social conventions. In Soddy's (1922, p. 27) words, 'Capital merely means unearned income divided by the rate of interest and multiplied by 100.'

The logical contradiction between unlimited growth of debt and limited growth of real wealth is translated into a social conflict between the *rentiers* (interest recipients) and workers. The conflict will take the form of debt repudiation. Debt grows at compound interest and as a purely mathematical quantity encounters no limits to slow it down. Wealth grows for a while at compound interest, but, having a physical dimension, it sooner or later encounters limits to further growth. The positive feedback of compound interest leads to explosive growth of debt, which is met by counteracting defensive actions of debt repudiation, that is, inflation, bankruptcy, confiscatory taxation, fraud, theft – all of which breed violence. Conventional wisdom considers the latter pathological, but accepts compound interest as normal. Logic demands, however, that we constrain compound interest in some way, or accept episodic debt repudiation as a normal and necessary adjustment. Of course inflation, bankruptcy, fraud, and so on can happen also as a result of straightforward corruption or incompetence. But the point is that exponential growth of debt will eventually force such occurrences even in the presence of normal honesty and competence.

Soddy (1926, p. 198) paraphrases J.M. Keynes's 1923 discussion of the value of the French franc: the purchasing power of money is settled in the long run by the proportion of his earned income that the worker permits to be taken from him by the *rentier* (understood here as debt-holder). It will continue to fall until the commodity value of money due to the *rentier* falls to that proportion of the national income which, in Keynes's words, 'accords with the habits and mentality of the country' – or the habits and mentality of the growing world, in Soddy's para-phrase. We understand this to mean that the growth of a *rentier* class living on interest from debt will eventually require the transfer of more income from workers than they will tolerate, resulting in conflict and debt repudiation, usually by inflation, because money debt can grow faster than the production of real wealth.[10]

Money should not bear interest as a condition of its existence, but only when genuinely lent by an owner who gives up its use while it is in the possession of the borrower. When the commercial banking system lends money it gives up nothing, creating the deposits *ex nihilo* up to the limit set by the reserve requirement. There is an opportunity cost to the bank in the sense that if it lends to A it forgoes the opportunity of making the same loan to B. There is an opportunity cost in allocating the virtual wealth among alternative borrowers, but there is no oppor-tunity cost to the bank in acquiring the virtual wealth in the first place. Unlike an individual, when a bank lends money it does not abstain from spending that money for the duration of the loan. The burden of abstinence is borne by the public.

The real lender is the community, which ends up holding more money debt and fewer real assets. In other words, the community has abstained from use of real assets, making these available to the bank's borrower in exchange for the money created by the bank and loaned to the borrower. If the community does not want to hold any more money and tries to convert the additional money into real assets, it simply bids up the price of real assets, thus lowering the real value (purchasing power) of its money holdings, the difference going to the banks which created the new money. If the community's demand for virtual wealth has not yet been satisfied, then the community lends voluntarily by holding the extra money and fewer assets. If it does not want to hold the extra money, it lends involuntarily by bidding up prices and reducing the purchasing power of its money holdings to 'make room' for the new money that the borrower received. In either case a part of the community's virtual wealth is transferred from the public to the issuer of new money. We know the new money will be spent and increase demand because the borrower would not pay interest for it if he did not intend to spend it. Prices are eventually bid up since *ex nihilo* creation of money (demand) is easier and faster than *ex materia* creation of new physical wealth (supply). The very existence of the bulk of our money now depends on this debt never being retired, only continuously rolled over. The existence of money has become a source of private income, and its total supply becomes a 'concertina', expanding to fuel a boom (when loans are in demand), and contracting to reinforce a slump (when there is little demand for new loans). The mere fact that most of our money supply was loaned into existence and must be repaid at interest introduces an additional growth bias into the economy.

Soddy (1926, p. 296) summarized these issues by pointing out that modern bankers

> have been allowed to regard themselves as the owners of the virtual wealth which the community does *not* possess and to lend it and charge interest upon the loan as though it really existed and they possessed it. The wealth so acquired by the impecunious borrower is not given up by the lenders, who receive interest on the loan but give up nothing, but is given up by the whole community, who suffer in consequence the loss through a general reduction in the purchasing power of money.

A further contradiction arises from the practice of interest-bearing national debt being used as collateral security by bondholders when they borrow from commercial banks. The bank creates a deposit (new money) for the borrowing bondholder and charges him interest. The public is taxed to enable the government to pay interest on the bond to the bondholder who, in effect, passes the interest on to the bank. Soddy (1926, p. 298) draws the conclusion that

> taxes are being paid to the bank for doing what the taxes were imposed to prevent being done, namely, the increase of the currency. Otherwise, there would have been no reason for the State to borrow at interest if it had not wished to prevent the increase of the currency.

This is for Soddy the final *reductio ad absurdum* of the monetary system.

Soddy is important because he made a serious effort to reckon with problems of non-growth. Although he was an enthusiast of scientific progress and a believer in the possibility of abundance for all thanks to scientific and technical advance, he was nevertheless sure that this could never happen under an economic system that confused debt with wealth, and behaved as if growth in the latter would increase the former. His monetary reforms, to be discussed, were aimed at stopping money debt from behaving in ways that are impossible for wealth to behave. A first step away from a culture of exponential growth and toward a culture capable of dealing with problems of non-growth would be to restrict the ability of money to do some of the things that wealth cannot do. This seems to mean two things. First, limiting the indefinite exponential growth of money values implicit in projections of compound interest growth over long periods. Second, limiting the 'conjuror's trick' of creating money *ex nihilo* and then destroying it. That power would be taken away from the private banks, and reserved to the government.

Monetary reform

The comments of Lloyd Mints (1950, p. 4) help us to see why these issues are so vexed:

> If a malignant despot desired to create the utmost confusion among his subjects on questions of public policy, he would surely require that any question of importance invariably be considered jointly with at least one other, unrelated, problem; and if he had a real genius as his adviser, the latter would immediately suggest that joint discussion of private lending operations and monetary policy would serve the purposes of his master very nicely . . . With a sensible financial structure, these two problems would have nothing in common. It would seem that an evil designer of human affairs had the remarkable prevision to arrange matters so that funds repayable on demand could be made the basis of profitable operations by the depository institutions. It is wholly fortuitous that an income can be earned from the use of such funds, but this being so has resulted in the creation of institutions which have largely taken over the control of the stock of money, an essential governmental function.

Three basic reforms had been suggested by Soddy to make the separation later called for by Mints, and to restore honesty and accuracy to the function of money in the economic system:

1. a 100 per cent reserve requirement for commercial banks;
2. a policy of maintaining a constant price index;
3. freely fluctuating exchange rates internationally.

These policies remain very sensible even though the world has changed much in the half century since they were suggested.

With a 100 per cent reserve requirement the commercial banking system could no longer create and destroy money. That basic privilege, along with the seigniorage prerogative and the ownership of virtual wealth, would be restored to the State, which would again become the sole 'utterer' of money. Banks would have to exist by charging for their 'legitimate' services, that is, those that do not require the creation of money – for example, safekeeping, chequing and clearing of payments, and lending at interest the real money of real depositors (savings or time deposits, not demand deposits). Financial intermediation (lending other people's money) would no longer have any connection with the supply of money, and the wealth lent by the intermediary would be wealth whose use had been forgone by some depositor for the period of the loan. Every increase in expenditure by borrowers would be matched by an act of saving or abstinence on the part of a depositor, rather than by the private appropriation of part of the virtual wealth of the community.

Frank Knight (1927) fully approved of this recommendation, noting in support that

> it is absurd and monstrous for society to pay the commercial banking system 'interest' for multiplying several fold the quantity of medium of exchange when (a) a public agency could do it at negligible cost, (b) there is no sense in having it done at all, since the effect is simply to raise the price level, and (c) important evils result, notably the frightful instability of the whole economic system.

Knight might have added that the public agency would not only incur negligible costs of production of the new money, but would also enjoy considerable seigniorage profits.

Three reasons for 100 per cent reserves have been given in the literature. First, to prevent private banks from creating money, so that the government could exercise more effective control. Through its increased direct control of money government would be able to exert stronger indirect effects on employment, national income and inflation. Everyone recognizes that inflation is mainly a monetary phenomenon, but the Monetarist School would go farther and claim that employment and national income are strongly influenced by the money supply as well. Second, 100 per cent reserves would prevent panics and runs on banks – an alternative to the FDIC which has problems of 'moral hazard', to be considered later. Third, the 100 per cent reserve requirement would recapture the use of virtual wealth and seigniorage for public purposes, thereby reducing the need for government borrowing at interest to finance public works. Following Soddy, we have emphasized the third reason, although most discussions emphasize the first and second reasons (Barber, 1973).

If the State is then to be the sole issuer of money, what principle will guide it in determining how much money to put into circulation?

Money would be created or destroyed by the State as necessary in order to keep the purchasing power of money constant. A price index, similar to but more comprehensive than the present Consumer Price Index, would be devised by a national statistical authority. If the index shows a tendency to fall over time, the government will finance its own activities by printing new money. Alternatively it might lower taxes, or use newly minted money to repurchase interest-bearing national debt. In other words, deflation would be corrected by some form of money-creating government deficit. If the index shows a rising tendency, the government will raise taxes, or issue interest-bearing national debt, and *not spend* the revenue so raised. Inflation would be corrected by a money-destroying government surplus. The price index would function analogously to a thermostat, or a governor on a steam engine. It would provide a mechanism for negative or stabilizing feedback. By contrast, the fractional reserve banking system provides destabilizing or positive feedback since the money supply expands during a boom and contracts during a slump, thereby reinforcing the original tendency. Also, to the extent that banks issue money in an inflationary boom and receive net repayments in a deflationary slump, they tend to be repaid in dollars of greater purchasing power than the dollar lent.

In the language of the 'rules versus authority' debate in monetary policy the constant price index falls in the category of a rule, and was advocated as such by Henry C. Simons (1948), the founder of the Chicago School. Rules have the advantage of being clear and known by all, thus diminishing the uncertainty of business expectations, whereas the actions of authorities are unpredictable and subject to political influence and error of judgement. Exactly what the rule should be (constant money supply, constant rate of growth in money supply, or constant price index), is of less importance than the adoption of *some* rule. The obvious virtue of the rule of a constant price index is fairness over time – the avoidance of the well-known problems of inflation and deflation.

We are aware of the technical problems of constructing index numbers, their tendency to 'wear out' over time as consumption patterns change, leading to the need to alter weights; the problem of measuring change in terms of beginning weights or ending weights, and so on. However, a reasonable consumer price index already exists, and we do routinely measure inflation adequately if not ideally, so this is nothing new. The difficulty of controlling that index by policy, because of lags, and changes in velocity of circulation of money are acknowledged, but again are problems we already have to face under the present arrangements. Certainly there would be much less slippage in monetary control with 100 per cent reserves.

A more serious difficulty is the existence of 'near or quasi-money', for example credit cards or highly liquid assets so easily convertible into money that individuals tend to treat them as money in making their plans. The existence of near money blunts the instrument of monetary policy. Financial deregulation has led to the practice of chequing deposits being created by unregulated institutions. Clearly, if one is to control the bank's ability to create money, it will not do to allow non-bank private institutions to begin creating money. But that, again, is as much a problem for the existing system as for the alternative we are suggesting.

Since international flows of gold, the monetary base in Soddy's day, would play havoc with any policy of maintaining the internal price level constant, it was necessary to propose insulating internal policy from the vagaries of the international balance of payments. This would be accomplished by a freely fluctuating exchange rate which would automatically attain equilibrium in the balance of payments at a market rate which, presumably, would reflect a purchasing-power parity between national and foreign currencies. International gold flows and the consequent inflationary and deflationary pressures on the national currency would be eliminated. Since the 1920s, freely fluctuating exchange rates have more or less come into being, but it is important to see their role in the context of Soddy's overall policy, and to remember that Soddy was proposing flexible exchange rates at a time when most economists were firmly wedded to the gold standard.

Unlike Soddy, I do not regard these three policies as a panacea. Nevertheless I believe that tightening the coupling between the real economy and its symbolic monetary control system is very important. If money debt is not allowed to expand without the simultaneous expansion of credit – that is, if a lender somewhere must actually forego the use of every dollar that a borrower somewhere else spends – then the expansion of debt would be brought more into line with the realistic possibilities for the expansion of wealth. One would expect this identity of one person's credit with another person's abstinence to lead to more conservatism in lending. If someone actually has to give up the money which the borrower receives, many more relevant questions will be asked about the nature of the project and the character and competence of the borrower. This greater demand for information regarding creditworthiness may give the edge to smaller, more locally based financial intermediaries, especially if they are no longer in competition with banks whose money-creating ability confers an advantage on bigness.

Borrowing in general would come under greater scrutiny. For example, conservative housing mortgage lending would look better relative to lending to finance leveraged buyouts or foreign currency speculation.

If it is felt that this would be too conservative and that the virtual wealth of the community should be available to finance loans, then the government could set up lending institutions and engage in net lending or net retirement of loans by simple creation and destruction of money as dictated by changes in the price index. We think, however, that the first claim on virtual wealth (or seigniorage) would be to directly finance public investment without taxing or borrowing. Avoidance of borrowing also avoids future transfers from taxpayers to bondholders. Of course the ability of the government to do this is limited by the tendency of the price index to rise once the value of such public investment exceeds the virtual wealth of the community. But at least the virtual wealth of the community would be used by the community (the State) rather than the private banking sector. We see an analogy here with Henry George's proposal that land rents should be captured for public purposes. Neither land nor money is the creation of individual labour or initiative. Both are fundamental bases of community, and revenues generated from them are more appropriately treated as community rather than private income.[11] If public revenues were raised more from these community sources, it would be possible to tax individual labour and initiative at lower rates, thereby reducing the incentive-dampening effects of our present system of taxation.

According to a study by the Federal Reserve Bank of St Louis (Neumann, 1992), seigniorage in the USA has averaged annually over the past forty years about 2 per cent of annual federal expenditures. This concept of seigniorage is the profit yielded from the government's monopoly in issuing base money (that is, reserves plus currency in circulation). Since seigniorage is by definition profit accruing *to the government*, it is calculated in the literature as profit on the creation only of that part of the money supply which the government itself directly creates, namely, 'the monetary base rather than the creation of deposits by private depository institutions' (Neumann, 1992, p. 30). Yet, as we have seen, the private commercial banks multiply reserves by roughly a factor of ten. So it would seem, as a first approximation, that the 'private seigniorage', or if that term is a definitional contradiction, 'the private profit from monetary creation analogous to seigniorage', should be about ten times the seigniorage on the monetary base, or about 20 per cent of federal revenues.

As a second approximation, however, we must make two corrections. First, actual reserve requirements are closer to 3 per cent than to our numerical example of 10 per cent (the latter applies only to accounts above \$46.8 million; those below that amount, surely the majority, require only 3 per cent). Therefore the actual multiplier would be closer to $1/0.03 = 33$, than to 10. The other correction takes account of the fact that only part of base money (reserves, not currency in circulation) is multiplied by the factor of 33.[12] The 2 per cent of federal expenditures estimate of seigniorage includes seigniorage on currency in circulation as well as on reserves held by commercial banks. If base money were half reserves and half currency in circulation, then our estimate of private bank seigniorage would be half of 2 per cent, or 1 per cent, times 33, or 33 per cent of public expenditures. Surprisingly, it seems that reserves are currently only about one-sixth of base money, so that private seigniorage would be about $1/6 \times 2$ per cent $\times 33 = 11$ per cent. Reclaiming public ownership of virtual wealth by instituting 100 per cent reserve requirements, while not a financial panacea, yields a significant (probably between 11 per cent and 33 per cent of public expenditure) increase in public revenue. These estimates are crude and serve only to establish that the private seigniorage, while not enormous, is not trivial either.

The 'private seigniorage' of commercial banks is such an obvious analogue to government seigniorage on reserves that it is quite surprising that we find neither mention nor calculation of it in the literature. Nor do we find 'private seigniorage' recognized in the money and banking chapters of the basic textbooks, although they all describe how banks create money. In the case of a single monopoly bank the private seigniorage would all be bank profit. In the case of a purely competitive banking sector the private seigniorage would be competed away in lower fees or higher deposit rates of interest, like excess profit in any purely competitive market with free entry. In either extreme case, or in the more realistic in-between case, the government can still convert the private seigniorage into true government seigniorage by moving to a 100 per cent reserve system. Obviously, the 100 per cent mark could be approached gradually over time by raising the reserve requirement a few percentage points per year.

It was argued earlier that money has a tendency to foster the exponential-growth culture by inducing the fallacy of misplaced concreteness. It does this in two ways. First, by virtue of the fact that money can be created out of nothing and can grow for ever, it seduces us into thinking that wealth, for which it is a symbol, can also do these things. Second, by allowing the historical shift from simple commodity production $(C-M-C^*)$ to capitalist circulation $(M-C-M^*)$ it focuses our attention on abstract exchange value, the accumulation of which appears to be unlimited, and away from concrete use value, the increase of which is clearly limited by our capacity to use the items accumulated.

The policy proposals derived from Soddy do not abolish the exponential-growth culture – they do not directly forbid or even limit the existence of compound interest. But 100 per cent reserve requirements would seem indirectly to slow the exponential-growth culture more than any other financial measure that we can currently think of. Other policies for physically limiting throughput have been discussed elsewhere in this book, and these are, we think, better measures for combating the consequences of exponential growth than trying indirectly to control throughput by controlling money. Nevertheless, the behaviour of money and the real economy should become more congruent. One hundred per cent reserves is a step in that direction. In addition, perhaps a general shift in investments from interest-earning assets to dividend-earning equities would be worth promoting. Dividends are variable, *ex post* earnings based on real experience, whereas interest-bearing assets are *ex ante* promises based on expectations which become unrealistic if projected very far into the future.

But what if wealth expands with no expansion in the money supply – would that not make commerce more difficult? Perhaps, but it would soon lead to a fall in prices, which would be the signal for the government to put more money in circulation so as to maintain the price index constant. The main reason for the constant price index is to maintain fairness between creditors and debtors over time, and to avoid the multiple injustices of a rubber yardstick – not a fear that commerce could not be effected with less money relative to goods and services. The amount of virtual wealth held voluntarily by the community will automatically adjust with the population, income level, and payments habits of the community – and that adjusted amount of virtual wealth will be divided up among as many dollars as are in circulation. Current transactions can be conducted in pennies or in dollars and there is no problem (assuming flexible prices). But if debtors have to pay back in dollars that today are worth a hundred times more (or less) than when they borrowed the dollars, problems arise.

Under 100 per cent reserve requirements there would be far less need for the Federal Deposit Insurance Corporation, and the perverse incentives that it gives to banks and depositors alike to accept risky loans. The single rule of 100 per cent reserves would make a lot of other banking regulations unnecessary. The feared failure of a few large banks would not cause a multiple failure of other banks as a result of a cascading loss of deposits and monetary contraction. Therefore the 'too big to be allowed to fail' doctrine that has governed recent banking regulation would lose most of its rationale. This doctrine in effect extends government 'insurance' to stockholders and managers of the banks, as well as to depositors, greatly increasing what economists call 'moral hazard' – that is, the incentive to seek high returns by taking greater risks than prudent because someone else will have to pay for the loss.

Moral hazard: recent financial experience

Another way of defining moral hazard is that it is what results from the combination of privatized profit and socialized loss. In the words of Kenneth A. Guenther (quoted in Greider, 1987), Executive Vice President of the Independent Bankers Association of America, 'The combination of interest rate deregulation with 100% deposit insurance is like the invention of gunpowder – sooner or later it was bound to explode.' But deregulation of banking and finance was all the rage under Reagan, and the banking sector wanted 'the government off its back'. Nowadays the last thing it wants is for the government to leave the scene of the train wreck. Ironically, the degree of government involvement in the financial sector through the Resolution Trust Corporation in its clean-up operations is proving much greater than before. Some Savings and Loan Institutions are making sweetheart deals to buy repossessed thrifts at bargain prices – and are thereby gaining, at government expense, huge competitive advantages over those S&Ls that were well managed and survived the storm. The latter still have some bad loans on their books, unlike the born-again S&Ls whose sins were all forgiven by the grace of the government as part of the inducement to the prospective buyer. Those deemed 'too big to be allowed to fail' are of course especially favoured, further encouraging bigness.

The diminished aversion to risk under the conditions of moral hazard also led US commercial banks to invest heavily in the South (Third World), and thereby contributed to the international debt crisis. One of the reactions to that crisis was for the USA and other Northern creditors to pressure the multilateral development banks to lend more to the South so that the South could pay its debts to Northern commercial banks. Since, under fractional reserve banking, prevention of Northern commercial bank failure is, to a considerable degree, really in the public interest, this was not an unreasonable thing to do. This was one of the reasons for the increased use of so-called fast-disbursing structural adjustment loans by the World Bank, discussed below in the next section on international finance.

Moral hazard seems pervasive in the financial world. Does it result from the failure to recognize that wealth cannot grow as fast as debt?

Keynes said that whatever is physically possible ought, with a bit of imagination, to be financially possible. Have we converted this sound dictum into its fallacious inverse, that whatever is financially possible, or even convenient, must be physically possible? The more difficult physical growth becomes as we encounter limits, the harder we try to push the alternatives of financial growth, and growth by merger and global integration. Attempts to encourage increasingly difficult growth with all sorts of guarantees and incentives leads to moral hazard. Moral hazard is one more force pushing us towards debt repudiation as an episodic readjustment of the financial world to the real world. Unfortunately, that repudiation, however logically unavoidable, will be unjust and probably violent.

The dangers of international finance
Economics for community is under special threat from the international nature of finance. Money flows around the world far more freely than labour, or means of production, or even products. This flow profoundly influences where production will occur and the economic prospects for different parts of the world. It will not be possible to develop stable regional or national economies if regions or nations have no control over the movement of money.

Current trends, unfortunately, are weakening national control. Until now many Third World countries have recognized that their ability to function as independent nations depends on having some financial institutions of their own. They have, therefore, protected these against outside competition. However, a major innovation in the Uruguay Round of the General Agreement on Tariffs and Trade (GATT) is to forbid such practices. Countries failing to subject their institutions to competition with international banks and insurance companies would be penalized by restrictions on their trade in goods. If the new GATT is implemented as now proposed, the great international financial institutions will wipe out local banks and insurance companies in much of the world.

Twenty years ago the greatest power over the global economy may have been located in transnational corporations engaged in production. Today that power has shifted to insitutions dealing with finance. Investment has come increasingly to mean the buying and selling of productive enterprises rather than their establishment or expansion.

Money can also be made on speculation in national currencies. Huge sums can be moved intantaneously around the world to take advantage of even minor fluctuations in exchange rates and interest rates. Our view is that finance should serve productive enterprise and not be siphoned off into speculation. Even a small tax on financial transactions would inhibit this useless speculative churning.

On the other hand, such a tax would do little to discourage the massive speculative attacks mounted on currencies that are considered overvalued. As long as currencies are artificially valued in international exchange, such attacks will continue, and when they succeed (as against Great Britain and Italy), huge profits are reaped by the speculators at the expense of the general public. The best way to end this form of speculation is to adopt freely fluctuating exchange rates.

The chief argument against floating currencies is that the extra risk in international trade resulting from exchange rate fluctuations is a deterrent to trade, specialization, capital mobility and world economic integration. Flexible exchange rates do not prevent the lending and borrowing associated with trade, but they provide faster feedback and a corrective mechanism for overborrowing. When loans must be repaid in a foreign currency, the extra demand for that currency will drive up its price. This will make imports more difficult and exports easier, thus increasing the net amount of foreign currency earned, and reducing the real consumption of the debtor in a visible way. This can lead to less borrowing and reduced dependence on trade.

Whereas most economists and policy makers regard any impediment to integration of the global economy as bad, readers of this book will find arguments to the contrary in other chapters. There are highly destructive consequences for human community and for the natural environment resulting from policies that aim to replace national and regional economies by a globally integrated one. Since global integration has already gone too far, we welcome the deterrent effects of flexible exchange rates on further economic integration.

Better than globalization is a policy of balanced trade – that is, that current exports should pay for current imports, and that capital transfers (debts) between nations should be relatively small. At present, unfortunately, it is the capital account that dominates in the foreign exchange markets, and much of this is short-term debt whose frequent international movement is motivated by speculation rather than real investment. Limits to the degree of acceptable imbalance in the trade account would automatically limit the capital account imbalance, and vice versa. Perhaps a limit on capital transfers would be the best way to enforce a move toward balanced trade.

Long-term international debts contribute even more visibly to the harsh effects of international finance, especially in the Third World. In the 1970s Third World countries borrowed heavily from commercial banks in the USA and other Northern Hemisphere countries. The

theory was that this money would be invested in productive development that would produce profits from which it could be repaid. In fact
much of the money was invested unwisely, spent on projects with no
economic benefit, or taken for private purposes.

When it became clear in the 1980s that earnings from these 'investments' would not suffice for repayment, creditors began to pressure
multilateral development banks to speed up their lending to the South
in order to provide them with the foreign currency necessary to pay
their debts to Northern commercial banks. This was one of the reasons
for the increased use of so-called fast-disbursing structural adjustment
loans by the World Bank. These were also part of a general shift from
project-based to policy-based lending. The rationale was that efficient
projects frequently fail because of macroeconomic irrationalities, and
that the World Bank was pouring money down the sink to invest in
projects that were merely islands of temporary efficiency in a sea of
permanent irrationality.

Since the World Bank and IMF are dogmatically certain about what
the rational macroeconomic policies are (removal of subsidies, deficit
reduction, trade liberalization and privatization, which together constitute 'structural adjustment'), there need be no delays with lengthy study
and preparation as in the case of projects, and the loans can move the
money quickly. If an efficient policy increases output by more than
the interest on the loan, then the country is made better off, at least in
conventional terms of more production, just as with any loan. One may
ask, however, why it is necessary to borrow money to enact more
efficient policies. In part structural adjustment loans were necessary to
induce countries to enact policies that the World Bank and IMF were
sure would be good for them, while the countries themselves were not
so sure. Even if the borrowing government agreed, the World Bank
and IMF needed something to help sell the idea politically, so the loan
takes on some aspects of a bribe. Also it can make good sense to
borrow for policy reform, if the reform measures cut needed revenues,
as for example lowering tariffs would do. So, if one is sure that lowering
tariffs is a good policy, then it could make sense to borrow to compensate for lost revenues until new sources could be devised. Of course, it
might also make sense first to devise the new sources of revenue before
reducing tariffs and thereby avoid borrowing. But not borrowing would
mean no inflow of foreign exchange with which to meet payments to
the Northern private banks.

The correct decision depends on the interest rate and the productivity
of the policy reform. The first is known, but the latter is not. There is
in practice not even an attempt to estimate a rate of return for policy

loans because it is too intangible. Similarly, no such estimate is made for education and public health loans. In all of these cases it is felt that the theory is solid enough to go ahead without empirical reconfirmation in each case. However, education and public health have a direct and clear connection to welfare independently of their indirect connection via increased productivity, whereas policy reform has no direct welfare benefits and depends for its justification entirely on the presumed correctness of the indirect effects indicated by neoclassical economic theory. In the background was the awkward need to move foreign exchange to the South so it could flow back as interest to Northern banks. This was necessary because the failure of a few big banks could cause a cumulative contraction of credit with disastrous consequences. Many banks with heavy Third World loans were too big to be allowed to fail under our fractional reserve banking system.

Part of the willingness to forego the cost–benefit calculation of rate of return on these loans no doubt derived from the knowledge that such calculations can be, and frequently are, 'cooked' to give whatever answer is desired. So the sacrificed empirical test was not such a great change in the *de facto* mode of operation. But is not the World Bank concerned about getting repaid, and would that not lead it to be careful in making loans, at least according to its own best understanding? The fact is that the World Bank will almost always be repaid, even if the project or policy it finances produces only losses. This is because the Bank lends to sovereign governments which have the power to tax and print money. They cannot print foreign exchange, but they can buy it by printing more of their own money and accepting the consequences of inflation and devaluation – or they can tax their people honestly rather than by inflation. In either case they can pay back the World Bank, and nearly always will do so rather than default and lose their credit rating.

The World Bank will in fact be among the first creditors paid. Add to this the following facts: politicians love to borrow large amounts of money; the World Bank is under pressure to lend more since repayment flows on past loans are now so large that there is a 'negative net flow' of funds to the South from the Bank; its loan officers are evaluated in part by the amount of money they move – and we can see why the quality of the World Bank's portfolio has declined in strictly conventional terms (Wapenhans Report, 1992). The quickest way for a World Bank employee to become unpopular is to slow down the money pump, even if it is by demonstrating irrefutably that a certain loan is stupid. In an institution that stood to lose money from stupid behaviour such demonstrations would be rewarded rather than punished. We can also see why the situation bears all the hallmarks of 'moral hazard'.

What should the World Bank do? Slow down, devote a larger share of resources to project supervision, make smaller loans, perhaps take an equity position in some projects, or share in the losses to some extent. The latter would help overcome the moral hazard problem, and would probably improve project supervision. More vigorous adversarial review of projects internally would help, as would a shift in personnel evaluation criteria from meeting lending targets to actual project performance. More fundamentally, as has been argued elsewhere (Goodland et al., 1992), the World Bank should focus more on investing in natural capital restoration, in resource efficiency, and in domestic production of basic goods and services for local use under local control. This implies a substantial departure from the current export-led model of development with its celebration of foreign investment, with specialization and trade according to comparative advantage. At the present it seems that the World Bank and IMF are determined to apply the same failed policies to the new democracies of the former Soviet Union, and the now failing 'miracle economies' of Thailand and Southeast Asia.

Notes

1. This is the allocative efficiency criterion for investments, and does not imply sustainability. The latter must be guaranteed by a separate criterion.
2. As noted by James Tobin (1987, p. 275): 'It is after all, historical accident that supplies of transaction media in modern economies came to be byproducts of the banking business and vulnerable to its risks.'
3. The chain of redepositing and relending is represented mathematically by the infinite series: $1 + (1-r) + (1-r)^2 + (1-r)^3 + \ldots + (1-r)^n = 1/r$.
4. Kauffman (1986) provides the best single source on Soddy's work, both as chemist and economist.
5. Soddy's notion of virtual wealth bears a close resemblance to the 'fiduciary issue' described in the earlier quote from James Tobin.
6. It is possible that money could be issued by states or cities rather than by the nation, and this might be a means of promoting localism. If economic decentralization should proceed far enough, local monies should be considered, but in this essay we will treat money only at the national level of community.
7. As Soddy (1926, p. 228) put it,

   > The old extreme *laissez-faire* policy of individualistic economics jealously denied to the state the right of competing in any way with individuals in the ownership of productive enterprise, out of which monetary interest or profit can be made, and this was ignorantly extended even to the virtual wealth of the community.

8. In Soddy's words (1926, p. 153),

   > Psychologically the economic aim of the individual is, always has been, and probably always will be, to secure a permanent revenue independent of further effort, proof against the passage of time and the chance of circumstance, to support himself in old age and his family after him in perpetuity. He endeavors to do so

166   *On money*

by accumulating so much property in the heyday of his youth that he and his heirs may live on the interest on it in perpetuity afterwards. Economic and social history is the conflict of this human aspiration with the laws of physics, which make such a perpetuum mobile impossible, and reduces the problem merely to the method by which one individual may get another individual or the community into his debt and prevent repayment, so that the individual or community must share the produce of their efforts with their creditor.

Many Americans seem to think that the money they contributed to Social Security all their lives exists as capital in a bank somewhere earning interest that will support them in their retirement. But all Social Security does is to give them a lien on future revenue produced by younger cohorts. This intergenerational debt could be repudiated. In fact, when the numerous baby boomers retire and are replaced by smaller cohorts of wage earners, most of whom will not realize the traditional expectation of being richer than their parents, some repudiation of this debt seems likely.

9. As Soddy expressed it (1926, p. 326):

    Capital, by saving to an indefinite extent the expenditure of time in human production, appears to afford a continuous revenue of wealth without further work, but the origin of the wealth produced is in the continued use of capital by human agents, not in the capital itself. There is no ethical principle to which to appeal, in order to equate the time spent in the accumulation against the continuous expenditure necessary to make it productive, or to determine the just division of the wealth produced as between the capitalist and the worker.

10. Between 1980 and 1991 in the USA, the gross federal debt grew at an annual compound rate of 13.3 per cent; consumer debt grew at 9.3 per cent and business debt at 7.8 per cent. Combined total debt grew at an average annual compound rate of about 10 per cent. During the same period GDP grew at less than half of that rate (Cavanagh and Clairmonte, 1992).

11. Dr Arthur Peel of Nunawading, Australia, publishes a short fortnightly paper called *Arthur's Seat*, dedicated to economic and monetary matters. In the June 1992 issue he recounts an interesting episode that occurred 175 years ago in the Channel Island of Guernsey. The islanders were in debt as a result of the Napoleonic Wars, and in need of infrastructure, especially a public market building. Not wanting to go further into debt, the authorities decided to print 4500 pounds of Guernsey notes and used them to pay for the building. After completion some 36 shops or stalls in the building were rented out. As rental payments were received a portion of them were burned by the government each year until the total burned was 4500 pounds. The debt was liquidated, or rather vaporized. No interest was ever paid, and rental payments on the shops continue as public revenue to the present day. This seems to us an instructive example of how the virtual wealth of the community can be used for the common good. We do not claim that the massive US debt could be redeemed by reclaiming virtual wealth, but nevertheless think that Mr Peel's historical parable merits reflection.

12. The effective reserve requirement may be less than 3 per cent since some deposits have no reserve requirement at all, up to a certain limit. For relevant statistics see *Federal Reserve Bulletin*, published monthly.

References

Barber, G. Russell Jr (1973), 'The One Hundred Percent Reserve System', *American Economist*, **17**, (1), pp. 115–27.
Cavanagh, John H. and Frederick F. Clairmonte (1992), 'US Finance Capitalism: The Tottering Empire', *Third World Economics*, no. 51, 16–31 October, pp. 17–20.

Daly, H.E. (1980), 'The Economic Thought of Frederick Soddy', *History of Political Economy*, **12**, (4).

Goodland, Robert, Herman Daly and Salah El Serafy (eds) (1992), *Population, Technology, and Lifestyles: The Transition to Sustainability*, Washington, DC: Island Press.

Greider, William (1989), *The Trouble With Money*, Knoxville, TN: Whittle Direct Books.

Hubbert, M. King [1976] 1992, 'Exponential Growth as a Transient Phenomenon in Human History', in H. Daly and K. Townsend (eds), *Valuing the Earth: Economics, Ecology, Ethics*, Cambridge, MA: MIT Press.

Kauffman, George B. (ed.) (1986), *Frederick Soddy (1877–1956)*, Boston, MA: Reidel Publishing Company. See also Trenn (1979); and Daly (1980).

Knight, Frank (1927), 'Review of Wealth, Virtual Wealth, and Debt', *Saturday Review of Literature*, p. 732.

Marx Karl (1867), *Capital*, vol. I, chs 2 and 3.

Millikan, R.A. (1930), 'The Alleged Sins of Science', *Scribner's Magazine*, **872**, pp. 119–30.

Mints, Lloyd (1950), *Monetary Policy for a Competitive Society*, New York: McGraw-Hill, p. 4.

Neumann, Manfred J.M. (1992), 'Seigniorage in the United States: How Much Does the US Government Make From Money Production?', *Review*, Federal Reserve Bank of St Louis, **74** (2), March/April, pp. 29–40.

Schumpeter, Joseph (1954), *History of Economic Analysis*, New York: Oxford University Press, p. 1114.

Simons, Henry C. (1948), *Economic Policy for a Free Society*, Chicago: University of Chicago Press, p. 238.

Sinsheimer, R.L. (1978), 'The Presumptions of Science', *Daedalus*, pp. 23–5.

Soddy, Frederick (1922), *Cartesian Economics: (The Bearing of Physical Science upon State Stewardship)*, London: Hendersons.

Soddy, Frederick (1926), *Wealth, Virtual Wealth and Debt (The Solution of the Economic Paradox)*, London; 3rd edn, Hawthorne, CA: Omni Publications, 1961.

Soddy, Frederick (1934), *Role of Money*, London.

Soddy, Frederick (1943), *The Arch Enemy of Economic Freedom*, London.

Tobin, James (1965), 'Money and Economic Growth', *Econometrica*, October, p. 676.

Tobin, James (1987), 'Financial Intermediaries', in John Eatwell et al. (eds), *The World of Economics (The New Palgrave)*, New York: W.W. Norton, pp. 261–78.

Trenn, Thaddeus J. (1979), 'The Central Role of Energy in Soddy's Holistic and Critical Approach to Nuclear Science, Economics, and Social Responsibility', *The British Journal for the History of Science*, **12**, p. 42.

Wapenhans Report (1992), *Effective Implementation: Key to Development Impact* (R92–125), Washington, DC: World Bank.

VII   On purpose

Introduction

A very important but neglected question for economists is: Are humans basically creatures or creators? Did a creator make us (no matter over how long a time period or by what particular process), or did we make up the idea of the creator out of the excess neuronal capacity of our hyperdeveloped brain whose evolution is fully determined by the mechanical processes of random mutation and natural selection? The modern intelligentsia believes the latter; traditional wisdom believes the former. I side with traditional wisdom, because I think the modern intelligentsia has gone totally crazy. I believe that we are fundamentally creatures, although special creatures with self-consciousness, mind, and limited creativity – we are indeed created in the image of God, but more faintly so than the agnostic intelligentsia paradoxically seems to believe. As creatures, our limited creativity is subject to the restraints imposed by the rest of the created order, namely: finitude, temporality, impossibility of creating or destroying matter/energy, impossibility of perpetual motion, impossibility of speeds faster than light, impossibility of spontaneous creation of living things from non-living things, and so on. Given these biophysical limits of creaturehood, plus the moral limits imposed by our responsibility as Creation's steward, it seems to me ironic in the extreme that we have built our economy on the premise that it must grow for ever, that there are no boundaries imposed by the rest of creation, either from its biophysical structure, or from our ethical responsibility as the 'creature-in-charge'. Why this feeble performance by the creature-in-charge? A.N. Whitehead (1925) offered a reason:

> A scientific realism, based on mechanism, is conjoined with an unwavering belief in the world of men and higher animals as being composed of self-determining organisms. The radical inconsistency at the basis of modern thought accounts for much that is half-hearted and wavering in our civilization . . . It enfeebles thought by reason of the inconsistency lurking in the background.

The enfeeblement of modern thought, noted by Whitehead, is evident today in the environmental movement, especially as it is promoted by biologists and ecologists. Their science and philosophy is mechanistic. No final causes or purposes are permitted into their neo-Darwinian world of random mutation and natural selection. This mechanical process, over long time periods, is held to explain all living forms including their brains, consciousness and thinking. That humans' conscious thought suggests to them the immediate reality of final cause and purpose must, in this view, be an illusion – an illusion which itself was selected because of the reproductive advantage that it by chance conferred on those under its influence. The existence of any species is an accident, and its continued survival is always subject to cancellation by random mutation and natural selection anywhere in the interdependent ecosystem. For people who teach this doctrine to sophomores on Monday/Wednesday/Friday, only to spend their Tuesdays/Thursdays and Saturdays pleading with Congress and the public to save this or that species (usually the one they wrote their dissertation on) is inconsistent. Naturally the public asks the biologists what purpose would be served by saving certain threatened species. Since neo-Darwinian biologists do not believe in purposes, ends or final causes, this is not an easy question for them to answer. They reveal the inconsistency that Whitehead saw lurking in the background by the feebleness and wavering half-heartedness of their answers. They tell us about biodiversity, and ecosystem stability and resilience, and about a presumed instinct of biophilia that we are supposed to have. But they are too half-hearted to affirm any of these concepts as an abiding purpose, and thereby question a fundamental assumption of their discipline. Consequently their appeals to the public are feeble. Even an unexamined and unworthy purpose, such as GNP growth for ever, will dominate the absence of purpose. Economists, for all their shallowness and ignorance of the natural world, will continue to dominate ecologists in the policy forum simply because they affirm a purpose while the ecologists do not – and logically cannot as long as they remain faithful neo-Darwinists. In neo-Darwinian terms, the survival value of neo-Darwinism has become negative for the species that believes it. The enfeebling inconsistency lurking in the background has come centre stage.

Ecological economics has for its first ten years focused on criticizing economics from the viewpoint of ecology. I believe that this has been necessary and worthwhile. Yet as noted above, ecologists too have their blind spots and professional deformations. Neo-Darwinism may have much to recommend it as a working hypothesis or research guide, but as a world-view it has the overwhelming deficiency of leaving no room for purpose of any kind, much less for a distinction between good and bad purposes. Teleology has been banished from the neo-Darwinian's mechanistic system. The mechanical push and pull of efficient causation is everything; the persuasive lure of final causation is not supposed to exist. *But it does exist.* And unless one recognizes its existence it is meaningless to talk about policy. Indeed, unless one can also distinguish good from bad purposes, better from worse states of the world, it is impossible to talk about policy, since if policy is anything it is a plan for moving the world from a worse to a better state. If there is no such thing as better and worse states of the world then all policy is silly – if indeed 'silliness' any longer has meaning in such a world.

Support for the thesis outlined in the preceding paragraph is found in the following three chapters which conclude the book. I conclude the book on this theme because I believe that a critical discussion of right purpose will have to be the central focus of ecological economics for the next decade, and ecologists are even less well equipped than economists to deal with it.

Reference
Whitehead, A.N. (1925), *Science and the Modern World*, New York: Macmillan, p. 76.

18 Review of Edward O. Wilson's, *On Human Nature* (Harvard University Press, 1978)*

Political economy has a deep and long-standing interest in the subject of human nature, although the topic is seldom explicitly discussed any more by modern economists. For this reason, as well as for the reason that a number of economists were quite taken with Wilson's earlier book, *Sociobiology*, one would expect that many economists would be found among the readers of *On Human Nature*. No doubt biologists and economists have much to learn from each other. But what, specifically, might economists and other social scientists learn from *On Human Nature*? One hopes that, after surveying the wreckage of Wilson's attempt to found a coherent view of the nature of man on the logical quicksand of scientific materialism, social scientists will be better able to resist the temptation to follow the same path.

The book begins and ends with a very logical and forthright presentation of the two central dilemmas facing modern man. In between a number of somewhat plausible evolutionary stories are told to explain altruism, aggression, religion (indeed *everything*) by one or another variation on the theme of genetic chance and environmental necessity. There are well-known problems with a theory that explains everything (including itself) and this leads Wilson to his discussion of the two dilemmas, wherein lies the chief virtue of the book. Wilson thinks, however, that he has, in the end, escaped or solved the dilemmas. In this he is totally mistaken. He leaves a logical hole a mile in diameter. It remains to spell this out in detail, with references.

The first dilemma is that

> we have no particular place to go. The species lacks any goal external to its own biological nature ... Traditional religious beliefs have been eroded, not so much by humiliating disproofs of their mythologies as by the growing awareness that beliefs are really enabling mechanisms for survival. Religions, like other human institutions, evolve so as to enhance the persistence and influence of their practitioners. (p. 3)

Wilson sees that,

* Published in *Review of Social Economy*, October 1979, pp. 241–4.

the danger implicit in the first dilemma is the rapid dissolution of transcendental goals toward which societies can organize their energies.

Of course Wilson is a scientific materialist and does not himself believe in transcendental goals, but he recognizes their important role in the social order, even if illusory. Rather than base our society on such transcendental illusions Wilson suggests that we

> [s]earch for a new morality based upon a more truthful definition of man, [that we] dissect the machinery of the mind and – retrace its evolutionary history. (p. 4)

But this course will lead us, Wilson predicts, to *the second dilemma,*

> [w]hich is the choice that must be made among the ethical premises inherent in man's biological nature . . . science may soon be in a position to investigate the very origin and meaning of human values, from which all ethical pronouncements and much of political practice flow. (p. 5) . . . At some time in the future we will have to decide how human we wish to remain – in this ultimate, biological sense – because we must consciously choose among the alternative emotional guides we have inherited. (p. 6)

How are we to choose which emotional guides to follow and which to stifle? Wilson states the issue with precision:

> at the center of the second dilemma is found a circularity: we are forced to choose among the elements of human nature by reference to value systems which these same elements created in an evolutionary age now long vanished. (p. 196)

Our inherited value systems are a product of the earlier environment of the hunter-gatherer, and are not a reliable guide for the age of atomic power and genetic engineering. The difficulty is even more general: no moral value (indeed no rational thought at all) can be valid if it is fully explainable as the result of amoral or irrational causes. Random mutation and natural selection are irrational events, and although they can certainly explain much, they cannot explain rational and moral thought itself. Otherwise the theory of evolution would itself be merely a product of genetic chance and environmental necessity and would in the long run stand or fall not by its legitimate claim to be in large part true, but by its survival value, which Wilson implicitly admits is rather low because in his version the theory must undercut a belief in transcendental value, which, right or wrong, does have high survival value in providing a basis for social cohesion. If there is no supernatural or transcendental source of value which somehow makes contact with nature in the mind, or alternatively, if there is no providential force behind the genetic chance and environmental necessity of evolution, which would guarantee that past values were appropriate to future survival, then to what, besides chance or whim, can one appeal in choosing how to remake human nature?

That is the central logical issue to which Wilson's argument leads, and up to this point one must admire the hard-headed logical consistency of the scientific materialist at his best. Once a true dilemma such as this is encountered, once logic has been followed to its limit, one must make a leap of faith and take the consequences. There are two alternatives: affirm transcendental value as a reality to which we can turn for guidance; affirm the nihilism implicit in scientific materialism and give up all claim to truth or righteousness. Either affirmation involves a leap of faith.

Which leap does Wilson make? Neither! 'Fortunately,' he says (p. 196), 'this circularity of the human predicament is not so tight that it cannot be broken through an exercise of will.'

Now that is a remarkable escape act! Bound and gagged in a burning building, our hero, by an exercise of will, bursts his bonds and blows out the fire. But the problem lies not so much in the improbable plot as in the faulty logic.

There are two logical problems with the escape act.

First, where does 'will' come from for the scientific materialist who expects that

> [t]he mind will become more precisely explained as an epiphenomenon of the neuronal machinery of the brain. That machinery is in turn the product of genetic evolution by natural selection acting on human populations for hundreds of thousands of years in their ancient environments. (p. 195)

Is 'will' a part of the neuronal machinery? If so it is determined by past evolution and cannot suddenly overthrow its master. Or is 'will' an epiphenomenon? Strange epiphenomenon which can alter the basic phenomena! Where does 'will' come from? Could it be contraband smuggled into the land of scientific materialism from the land of transcendental value? Be that as it may, it has always seemed odd to me that the word 'epiphenomenon' should so habitually be applied to will, mind, or consciousness – the only things we experience directly, unmediated by the sometimes deceptive senses. Mind is what we know immediately and from the inside. It is the brain which we can only know from the outside and by means of the senses amplified by instruments.

The second problem is more fundamental. Let us pretend that the appeal to will is legitimate. The question remains whether what is demanded of will is legitimate. Can will break a *logical* circularity? Not even the most ardent believers in free will have ever claimed that one could evade a logical conclusion by an 'exercise of will'! One could understand how will might be appealed to as a general urge to action, but not as a criterion for deciding which action to take. Will may explain why we do in fact make moral judgements, but it does not help us to make the *right* moral judgement. The resolution of Wilson's second dilemma requires a criterion, not an urge. Not only does Wilson appeal to will while professing not to believe in it (except as an epiphenomenon), but he also requires the will to perform the miraculous tasks of breaking a purely logical circularity and serving as a criterion as well as an urge. This just will not do.

Ironically Wilson cautions that

[w]henever other philosophers let their guard down, deists can, in the manner of process theology, postulate a pervasive transcendental will. They can even hypothesize miracles. (p. 192)

From what has been said it is evident that Wilson has postulated a very mysterious 'exercise of will' of indeterminate (possibly transcendental!) origin, and has hypothesized that it can miraculously break out of logical circularities. Have deists let their guard fall so low? Not really. The whole issue here discussed was thoroughly laid to rest by C.S. Lewis in his 1946 classic, *The Abolition of Man*, and in chapter 3 of his book *Miracles* (1947) entitled 'The Self-Contradiction of the Naturalist'.

There was a time when the narrow-minded dogmatism of organized religion oppressed the force of reason as it was developing in the natural sciences. Are we beginning to witness a reversal of historical roles?

19 Beginning again on purpose: review of David Ehrenfeld's *Beginning Again: People and Nature in the New Millennium* (Oxford University Press, 1993)*

Gentle reader, study this book carefully even if you have to buy it for yourself. Ehrenfeld's crystalline English refracts the light of reason into its full spectrum of important facts, logical arguments, and true values. Intrusive management, world-class scholars, and state-of-the-art buildings whose windows do not open, are a few of the irritants around which his reflections form pearls. In the short space allotted to a reviewer I will share only a few of the many reasons for my enthusiasm for the book, as well as my one, but important, puzzlement.

As a twenty-year veteran and five-year refugee from academia I found the essays on university administration in the section appropriately titled 'Off Course' to be very much 'on target'. Ehrenfeld does not hold managers, especially in academia, in high esteem. The latter preside over large institutions whose main function is to seek meretricious 'prestige', while maximally absorbing public funds and carelessly forgetting past knowledge. The way for a university dean to succeed is not to encourage and facilitate good teaching and relevant research by the faculty, but to hire WCSLs (world-class scholars), or in Ehrenfeld's phonetic transliteration, 'wixels'. Wixels attract grants that carry large overhead disbursements to the university, making possible the payment of world-class managerial salaries. Of course wixels are not plentiful and most of them do not want to go to second-rate universities. No problem. Demand creates its own supply for wixels. An endowed chair with a high salary and the word 'distinguished' in its description automatically creates another wixel – maybe one of the new dean's old friends. Future grants facilitated by the added prestige may repay the disproportionate salary. However, if a university administrator fails to hire enough wixels, he or she can fall back on the strategy of constructing a state-of-the-art-building.

No wixel should ever teach. Teaching is reserved as punishment for those who prove to be non-wixel material. Certain subjects are not

* Published in *Conservation Biology*, **7** (3), September 1993, pp. 736–8.

177

conducive to becoming a wixel and are now generally not taught. Ehrenfeld lists classification of higher plants, marine invertebrates,
ornithology, and basically everything that is not genetics or molecular
biology. For economics the list of non-wixel knowledge scheduled for
planned forgetting includes history of economic thought, economic
history, comparative economic systems, and economic development –
basically anything that is not mathematical economics or econometrics.[1]
This process of forgetting usually means the jettisoning of specific,
concrete, descriptive knowledge in favour of any generalizable knowledge that can be reduced to a few first principles. While certainly
necessary, this quest for theoretical knowledge has become one-eyed,
eroding the very store of factual knowledge against which it should be
tested.

The best way to limit the growth of managerial idiocy is to reduce
the money flow that feeds it. So Ehrenfeld advises foundations to
restrict acceptable overhead charges to 10 per cent, and wealthy alumni
to exercise more critical judgement in giving. The latter are especially
cautioned not to trust the loyalty of university corporations to live up
to the terms of a bequest. I would add the advice to send your kids to
a liberal arts college instead of a university dedicated to the cloning of
wixels.

Now for my puzzlement. In his stimulating essay, 'The Roots of
Prophecy: Orwell and Nature', Ehrenfeld discusses the prophetic role
of George Orwell and notes that, unlike the Hebrew prophets, or
modern prophets such as C.S. Lewis and E.F. Schumacher, Orwell did
not believe in God. Ehrenfeld asks, 'If not the word of God, what was
the external standard that enabled Orwell to describe his world and
ours with such faithfulness to present and future reality?' An excellent
question. Ehrenfeld's answer is that 'Nature was his independent
standard . . .', and that the specific standards or values Orwell derived
from nature were honesty, reliability along with continuity/durability/
resilience, and beauty/serenity. Somehow these characteristics of nature
impressed Orwell more than their equally observable opposites. Let us
accept that this is a true statement about Orwell. If so, does it not mean
that Orwell was rather badly confused about the roots of his own
undoubted prophetic insight? When Ehrenfeld speaks of '*external* standard' and '*independent* standard', I assume he must mean, in the manner
of C.S. Lewis, external to nature. If so, these standards cannot be
derived from that to which they are external and from which they are
independent. Is this not the old 'naturalistic fallacy'?

I hasten to add that Ehrenfeld, himself a respectable modern prophet,
does not, as far as I can tell, derive his own standards from nature,

which he certainly knows better than Orwell did. In fact there are more than a few clues in the book to suggest that Ehrenfeld is more like C.S. Lewis and E.F. Schumacher in this regard than like Orwell – that is, he seems to draw his external standard not from nature, but apparently from the Judeo part of the same Judeo-Christian tradition whose Christian part was the external standard for Lewis and Schumacher. It is too late to ask Orwell about this, but Ehrenfeld is still alive and I hope continues in that condition for a long time, so I want to raise the question with him.

In case the fundamental importance of this question for conservation is not already obvious, let me share a story about a famous scientist testifying before Congress and urging government and religious leaders to supply the 'moral compass' that is needed to save the environment. Science, he argued, could do the rest, but the moral compass had to come from elsewhere. No naturalistic fallacy here – religion was explicitly asked to supply the compass. Yet this same scientist apparently holds to a cosmology in which there is no analogue to magnetic (objective) north! All is reducible to efficient or mechanical causation and there is no room for final causation, the lure of purpose, or objective value. What good is it to have a compass if there is no magnetic north to lure the needle toward itself? Or, to come at it from a different angle, biology teaches that all species share the same DNA, that we are all related and, by implication, that humans should love and preserve their relatives for reasons of intrinsic as well as instrumental value. The case for preserving biodiversity is based on an appeal to some combination of instrumental and intrinsic value. But biology also teaches that the whole show was a big accident and that all the differentiated parts, ourselves included, are little accidents, all produced by random mechanical causation with no purpose or final causation admitted. Is it possible, really, to love an accident? Is it possible to save what we cannot love? If biologists continue to insist that we must substitute the idea of 'Accident' for the idea of 'Creation', then they really undercut their own plea for the preservation of biodiversity beyond the most short-run instrumental arguments. If 'biophilia' is really genetically programmed into us, then why are we killing other species wholesale? This is not to deny the important role of chance and necessity, of evolution, in the practical working of Creation. But the assumption that the biologist's 'central dogma' is sufficient to require the substitution of Creation by Accident is past due for serious rethinking.

I said this was for me a puzzle, so do not expect a resolution. As A.N. Whitehead remarked, 'Scientists animated by the purpose of proving that they are purposeless constitute an interesting subject for study.' Biologist Charles Birch's book *On Purpose*, written from a Whiteheadian perspective, is the most helpful discussion of this problem that I have found, and I would be delighted if Ehrenfeld would review that book in *Conservation Biology*, or take some other occasion to shine the bright light of his intelligence and scholarship on this puzzle. If we are seriously to be engaged in 'Beginning Again', I hope that biologists will not, in their descriptions and explanations of the living world, abstract so completely from the immediate and universal experience of purpose that they are in the end left with no basis in their own science to support their pleas for political action to conserve biodiversity.

Note
1.   What is happening in the humanities under the influence of 'deconstructionist wixels' is left to others to recount, but in my second-hand opinion looks even worse than the corruption of the sciences and social sciences.

20 The cosmic purpose*

The environment and the economy are in mortal combat. Sustainable development is an effort to resolve this conflict. But why does the effort to deal with this impending Armageddon inspire such a low sense of urgency and ethical motivation in major institutions like the University, the Church, and most national governments? These institutions are certainly not protecting the earth from destruction in the manner of the four angels in *Revelation* 7:1, 'holding back the four winds of the earth so that no wind could blow on land or sea or against any tree'. Of course there are individual exceptions in each of these domains – prophetic voices that cry in the wilderness.

But why are these cries evoking so little response in so much wilderness? Is the Apocalypse of St John the Divine helpful in deeper ways than simply providing environmentalists with an ancient model of how to scare people into repentance with forecasts of doom? Is its message actually contrary to environmental preservation, as former US Secretary of the Interior, James Watt, thought? His logical argument was that if the end of the world is near, then it makes no sense to save anything for a non-existent beneficiary. Is there a more sane and hopeful message in *Revelation*? I believe there is, and will return to it in closing. But first I want to consider why this message of hope is so little heard today – and why our ears have become deaf to it.

Some very prominent US scientists, working overtime as prophets calling for environmental repentance, have asked themselves a related question about religion in general. Some of them have decided that science has the techniques, but is unable to ignite sufficient moral fervour to induce the public to accept and finance policies that apply these techniques. They thought that it would be worth a try to appeal to religion to supply the missing moral fervour as a basis for political consensus and action. This resulted, in May of 1992, in the 'Joint Appeal by Science and Religion on the Environment', led by the eminent scientists Carl Sagan, Edward O. Wilson and Stephen Jay Gould, along with a few religious leaders, and hosted by then Senator Al Gore.

The three scientists are quite well known not only for their highly informed and genuine concern about the environment, but also for their affirmations of scientific materialism and consequent renunciations of

* Published in *Resurgence*, July/August 1996.

any religious interpretation of the cosmos. What then was their rationale for courting the religious community? It was that while science presumably had the understanding on which to act, it lacked the moral inspiration to act and to inspire others to act. Or, in a frequently used metaphor, religion was asked to supply the moral compass and science would supply the vehicle.

I attended the conference, and was troubled at the time by what seemed to me a somewhat less than honest appeal by the scientists to a somewhat credulous group of religious leaders. A year or so later I read a book by a theologian, John F. Haught,[1] who had also been present, and discovered that he had precisely articulated my doubts.

Haught wondered aloud

> whether it is completely honest for them [the scientists] to drink in this case so lustily from the stream of moral fervour that flows from what they have consistently taken to be the inappropriate and even false consciousness of religious believers . . . the well-intended effort by the skeptics to co-opt the moral enthusiasm of the religious for the sake of ecology is especially puzzling, in view of the fact that it is only because believers take their religious symbols and ideas to be disclosive of the *truth* of reality that they are aroused to moral passion in the first place. If devotees thought that their religions were *not* representative of the way things *really* are, then the religions would be ethically impotent . . .
>
> It is hard to imagine how any thorough transformation of the habits of humans will occur without a corporate human confidence in the ultimate worthwhileness of our moral endeavours. And without a deep trust in reality itself, ecological morality will, I am afraid, ultimately languish and die. Such trust . . . must be grounded in a conviction that the universe carries a meaning, or that it is the unfolding of a 'promise'.

Haught's point, of course, is that Sagan, Wilson and Gould proclaim the cosmology of scientific materialism, which considers the cosmos an accident, and life within it to be no more than another accident, ultimately reducible to dead matter in motion. In their view there is no such thing as value in any objective sense, or purpose, beyond short-term survival and reproduction, which are purely instinctual, and thus ultimately mechanical.

One might reply that objective value does not exist externally, but is an internal affair created by humans and projected or imposed by humans on the external world. This is the solution of dualism, and has been dominant since Descartes, both in science and theology. Purpose, mind and value enter the world discontinuously in human beings; all the rest is mechanism.

Such a view, however, is contrary to the evolutionary understanding of kinship of human beings with other forms of life that is affirmed by science. For mind, value and purpose to be real, they must, in an evolutionary perspective, be present to some degree in the world out of which humans evolved, or else be the object of a special creation, which of course is not acceptable to science and the theory of evolution. Scientific materialism resolves the dilemma by denying the reality of purpose, mind and value in human beings as well as in the external world. The subjective feelings that we refer to as purpose or value are considered mere epiphenomena, ultimately explainable in terms of underlying physical structures and motions. The other resolution is to affirm that purpose and value is not a human monopoly, but is the basis of real kinship among species.

This alternative to scientific materialism, one that still takes science seriously, is worked out in the process philosophy of Alfred North Whitehead. This view is radically empirical. What we know most concretely and directly, unmediated by the sometimes deceptive senses or by abstract concepts, is our inner experience of purpose. That should be the starting point, the most well-known thing in terms of which we try to explain less well-known things. To begin with highly abstract concepts, such as electrons and photons, and explain the immediate experience of purpose as an 'epiphenomenon' incidentally produced by the behaviour of these abstractions, is an example of what Whitehead called the 'fallacy of misplaced concreteness'.

Gould himself has noted that 'we cannot win this battle to save species and environments without forging an emotional bond between ourselves and nature as well – for we will not fight to save what we do not love (but only appreciate in some abstract sense)'.[2] But is it possible to love an accident? More to the point, is it possible for an accident to love an accident? For an accident to fight to save another accident? I doubt it, but I do not doubt that it is possible for human beings who call themselves scientific materialists to fall in love with the world they study and come to know intimately.

God's world is lovable, and scientists often fall in love with it much more deeply than theologians! But should the scientists not confess that love and ask themselves how it is that they could have fallen in love with something their science tells them is an accident? In their daily life are they particularly fond of other random events? There is something fundamentally silly about biologists teaching on Monday, Wednesday and Friday that everything, including our sense of value and reason, is a purposeless product only of genetic chance and environmental necessity – and then on Tuesday, Thursday and Saturday trying to convince the public that they, who are themselves accidents, should love some other accidental piece of this purposeless world enough to fight and sacrifice to save it.

The absurdity is confirmed by the scientists' apparent inability to find anything to appeal to in their effort to rouse public support for the environment other than religiously based values that they themselves consider unfounded! Are they not trying to live by the fruit of the tree whose tap-root they are cutting? Is not our entire society, including the scientists, living off the depleting moral capital of traditional religious belief, just as surely as it is living off the depleting natural capital of the ecosystem?

To call the scientists' proposal 'quite ingenuous', as Haught does, is to be kind. It also should be surprising (and flattering beyond merit) to members of the religious community that the scientists should assume that the majority of today's religious people will in fact be led by their beliefs to care about the environment, when to date that has not happened. It is indeed a paradox that people whose professed beliefs give them no good reason to be environmentalists are usually trying harder to save the environment than are people whose beliefs give them every good reason to be environmentalists! The scientists are implicitly calling for a religious reformation, not just a moral compass that magically functions in an amoral universe – to point the scientists in the direction of public funds to save the environment.

As Alfred North Whitehead observed,

> Many a scientist has patiently designed experiments for the purpose of substantiating his belief that animal operations are motivated by no purposes. He has perhaps spent his spare time writing articles to prove that human beings are as other animals so that purpose is a category irrelevant for the explanation of their bodily activities, his own activities included. Scientists animated by the purpose of proving that they are purposeless constitute an interesting subject for study.[3]

We might add that religious persons animated by belief in a Creator God, yet happily participating in the destruction of Creation, also constitute an interesting subject for study.

In the discussions during the meeting in Washington DC of the Joint Appeal, the void of purpose was frequently glossed over in discussions with the phrase 'for our children'. But of course if we are accidents, then so are they, and the dilemma is not resolved by pushing it one generation forward. I recall that one lady was evidently so annoyed by the sentimentality of this often cloying invocation of 'our children', that she took the microphone to say that she had no children, and was she to understand, therefore, that she had no reason to care about the future of God's Creation? To read some biologists you would think that whoever does not manage to propel their genes into the next generation might as well never have lived.

Environmentalists and advocates of sustainable development really must face up to deep philosophical and religious questions about why their efforts ultimately make sense. Neither vague pantheistic sentimentality about Gaia, nor *ad hoc* wishful invention of instincts like 'biophilia' can withstand much philosophical criticism.

But they are welcome first steps away from pure scientific materialism. I find the ideas of a minority of Christian thinkers influenced by Whitehead, such as John B. Cobb, Jr, John F. Haught and Charles Birch, to offer a much more solid base than either scientific materialism or traditional theology for loving nature enough to fight to save it (in the sense of not provoking its premature demise).

Many other traditional religions share with Christianity a theology of creation (not the same as the literalist sect doctrine of 'scientific creationism'), so the theological basis for something like 'biophilia', as a persuasive virtue rather than a mechanical instinct, is by no means limited to Christianity. All traditional religions are enemies of the same modern idolatry – that accidental Man, through economic growth based on science and technology, is the true creator, and that the natural world is just a pile of instrumental building blocks to be used in furthering the arbitrary projects of one purposeless species. If we cannot assert a more coherent cosmology than that, then we might as well close the store and all go fishing – at least while the fish last.

The Revelation of St John is an affirmation of cosmic purpose and the unfolding of a promise projected to the end of time. We need that affirmation today. We no longer understand the imagery of apocalyptic literature, and consequently the book has become the happy hunting ground for crazed, literalist, would-be messiahs of whom David Koresh is only the most recent. I certainly sympathize with the Eastern Orthodox Church's early reluctance to admit *Revelation* to the canon. But its affirmation of cosmic purpose and of fulfilment of promise is crucial.

In fact, it is the denial of purpose, explicit both in modern scientific materialism and deconstructionism, that drives people to look for purpose wherever they can find it, underground, as it were. They no longer find it in science, or even the humanities – indeed especially not in the humanities under the thrall of deconstructionist nihilism. Universities have totally abdicated on questions of meaning and purpose. Mainline Churches have not abdicated, but are often so identified with the dominant culture that their affirmation seems muted. This frequently leaves fundamentalist sects as the only alternative to secular meaninglessness, and by default the only public defenders of the irrepressible recognition that purpose is real and that Creation carries with it a promise.

It is this message of hope in the purpose and promise of Creation that must be recaptured and proclaimed on the nineteen-hundredth anniversary of the *Book of Revelation*. Both science and Christianity believe that the world will end – even *Revelation*'s four angels at the four corners of the earth were only temporarily holding back the winds of destruction. Christianity affirms the hope and faith in God's promise that neither the world while it exists, nor its ultimate demise, is purposeless. Our main task is to reflect more deeply on our purposes and to align them with our best understanding of God's purposes.

To end the world prematurely by our own actions, I submit, is to usurp God's prerogative as much as if we insisted on trying to make the world everlasting or on reversing the entropy law. To despair of making the world last as long as possible, because it will all end some day no matter what we do, is to lose faith both in God's promise and in our direct intimate experience of purpose as part of ourselves and therefore of the cosmos to which we belong. It is analogous to an individual committing suicide rather than living life. To claim that the whole show is a purposeless exercise in random change leaves would-be environmentalists without a leg to stand on, and with a standing invitation to despair. In *Revelation*, after all the conflict, destruction and decay, God's promise is affirmed in the final vision, containing the same tree of life as in *Genesis*. This time there is no tree of knowledge of good and evil with its forbidden fruit – just the tree of life with its healing leaves.

Notes

1. John F. Haught, *The Promise of Nature: Ecology and Cosmic Purpose*, Mahwah, NJ: The Paulist Press, 1993. See also Charles Birch, *On Purpose*, Kensington, NSW, Australia: New South Wales University Press Ltd, 1980.
2. S.J. Gould, 'Unenchanted Evening', *Natural History*, September 1991, p. 14. For an insightful discussion see David Orr, *Earth in Mind*, Washington, DC: Island Press, 1994, chapter 20.
3. A.N. Whitehead, *The Function of Reason*, Princeton, NJ: Princeton University Press, 1929.

Index